Praise for

TEAM TOPOLOGIES

"*Team Topologies* provides fresh insights on how to anticipate and adapt to market and technology changes. To survive, enterprises need to unlearn existing command and control structures and instead move authority to leaders with the best information to take action and respond. This book will help executives and business leaders focus on the key strategies of high-performance teams to effectively address the needs of today and the evolving landscape of tomorrow."

—**Barry O'Reilly**, Founder of ExecCamp, Business Advisor, and
Author of *Unlearn* and *Lean Enterprise*

"There is nothing more fundamental to management than how you structure your organization and what behaviors you encourage. Despite this, few have attempted to catalog and analyze the organizational design patterns of IT organizations going through digital, DevOps, and SRE transformations. Skelton and Pais have not only accepted this bold challenge, but they've also hit the mark by creating an indispensable and unique resource."

—**Damon Edwards**, Co-Founder of Rundeck

"*Team Topologies* provides a much-needed framework for evaluating and optimizing team organization for increased flow. Teams that have the right size, the right boundaries, and the right level of communication are poised to deliver value to the company and satisfaction to the team members. *Team Topologies* combines a methodical approach with real-world case studies to unlock the full potential of your tech teams."

—**Greg Burrell**, Senior Reliability Engineer at Netflix

"*Team Topologies* by Matthew Skelton and Manuel Pais is unique. It is going to have a big influence across tech companies. We need a structured and methodical approach to shaping teams for continuous delivery instead of copying a few Spotify rituals. This is the book."

—**Nick Tune**, API Platform Lead, Navico

"At Condé Nast International, [the DevOps Topologies] was crucial in understanding our current DevOps state and in defining the vision for our aspirational DevOps operating model. We were able to navigate round the pitfalls and organizational anti-patterns as excellently described in the models....I am extremely pleased that Matthew and Manuel are growing on the success of the DevOps Topologies and turning their further learnings into the far-reaching book *Team Topologies* for organization design."

—**Crystal Hirschorn**, VP of Engineering, Global Strategy and Operations at Condé Nast

"The high-performing team is the core generator of value in the modern digital economy. But cultivating and scaling an adaptive ecosystem of such teams is a too-often elusive goal. In *Team Topologies*, Skelton and Pais provide innovative tools and concepts for structuring the next generation digital operating model. Recommended for CIOs, enterprise architects, and digital product strategists worldwide."

—**Charles Betz**, Principal Analyst, Forrester Research

"Matthew Skelton and Manuel Pais say '*Team Topologies* is meant to be a functional book'—and it is. It's well constructed and sign-posted, based in sound thinking, and challenges readers to assume, like them, that an organization is a sociotechnical system or ecosystem. From this assumption comes practical suggestions, no prescriptions, and skill in explaining an approach that provides for effective tech/human organization design. For anyone in the tech/organization design field, [*Team Topologies* is] well worth reading."

—**Dr. Naomi Stanford**, Organization Design Practitioner,
Teacher, and Author

"I have found Matthew and Manuel's work on patterns and language to be incredibly valuable in both shaping strategies to transform team contexts over time across our organization, as well as in helping business and technology leadership connect with the topics of flow and continuous delivery."

—**Richard James**, Head of Digital Technology &
Engineering at Nationwide

"Teams are the fundamental building block of organizations, how those teams work and the system they operate in are the difference between average and high performance. This book is a deep well of information for how you can optimize your organization's system for your current context."

—**Jeremy Brown**, Director, Red Hat Open Innovation Labs EMEA

"DevOps is great, but how do real-world organizations actually structure themselves to do it? You can't just put everyone on a single, silo-less team, all sitting together in one giant open-plan office and going out to lunch or playing foosball together. *Team Topologies* provides a practical set of templates for addressing the key DevOps question that other guides leave as an exercise for the student."

—**Jeff Sussna**, Founder & CEO, Sussna Associates, and
Author of *Designing Delivery*

"If you're looking for an analysis of the challenges with the traditional ways of working, and also some practical guidance on mitigation strategies (e.g., new interaction modes, reducing cognitive load, and creating appropriate 'Team APIs'), then this is the book for you!"

—**Daniel Bryant**, Technical Consultant/Advisor and
News Manager at *InfoQ*

"*Team Topologies* makes for a fascinating read as it explores the symbiotic relationship between teams and the IT architecture they support. It goes beyond the common approach of static org charts or self-organizing chaos and shows how to evolve the people system and IT system together."

—**Mirco Hering**, Global DevOps Lead Accenture and
Author of *DevOps for the Modern Enterprise*

TEAM TOPOLOGIES

ORGANIZING BUSINESS AND TECHNOLOGY TEAMS FOR FAST FLOW

MATTHEW SKELTON
and MANUEL PAIS

Foreword by Ruth Malan

IT Revolution
Portland, Oregon

25 NW 23rd Pl, Suite 6314
Portland, OR 97210

Cover and book design by Devon Smith

Library of Congress Catalog-in-Publication Data
Available upon request

ISBN: 978-1942788-812
eBook ISBN: 978-1942788-829
Kindle ISBN: 978-1942788-836
Web PDF ISBN: 978-1942788-843

For information about special discounts for bulk purchases, or for information
on booking authors for an event, please visit our website atITRevolution.com.

TEAM TOPOLOGIES

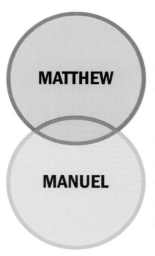

To my wife, Suzy Beck—for all your support and inspiration.

To Katie, my life partner and family stronghold—thanks for your tireless love and support.

To Dan and Ben, daily sources of warmth—hopefully this book can help you understand what Daddy does for a living.

CONTENTS

**PART III EVOLVING TEAM INTERACTIONS FOR INNOVATION
AND RAPID DELIVERY**

FIGURES & TABLES

FIGURES

TABLES

CASE STUDIES & INDUSTRY EXAMPLES

Chapter 8

FOREWORD

Keeping our systems small and simple is a worthy goal, yet it is also one that most successful systems defy. Lehman's laws of software evolution, and, in particular, continuing growth, captures the evolutionary pressure to add capabilities as systems are used and new demands or opportunities are perceived. Being able to cope with, and even harness, this increasing complexity raises the importance of dual design arenas: the design of systems and the design of the organization that creates and evolves systems. We have a considerable body of work focused on the former; that is, on systems and software design and architecture, including an ever growing number of books on domain driven design and software architecture. *Team Topologies* addresses the design of the software development organization, with Conway's law in view.

> The basic thesis [....] is that organizations which design systems [....] are constrained to produce designs which are copies of the communication structures of these organizations. We have seen that this fact has important implications for the management of system design. Primarily, we have found a criterion for the structuring of design organizations: a design effort should be organized according to the need for communication.[1]

The above quote from the conclusion of Mel Conway's classic paper on organizational design for software development is a most fitting beginning to this book. *Team Topologies* describes organizational patterns for team structure and modes of interaction, taking the force that the organization exerts on the system as a driving design concern.

As the complexity of the system increases, so, generally, do the cognitive demands on the organization building and evolving it. Managing cognitive load through teams with clear responsibilities and boundaries is a distinguishing focus of team design in the Team Topologies approach. To achieve duly scoped, bounded responsibilities, natural—and relatively independent—system (sub) structure is sought to align teams to. This takes Conway's law into account and leverages it to help maintain cohesive structures with clear boundaries and loose coupling (known as the reverse Conway maneuver, and described herein).

If this was the extent of it, *Team Topologies* would be a useful elaboration of Conway's paper, setting it in the current context. Of course, *Team Topologies* is even more than that. Notably, it identifies four team patterns, describing their outcomes, form, and the forces they address and are shaped by. Stream-aligned teams are the primary team form. These are teams that are optimized for flow, with all they need to effect continuous delivery of value and be fully responsive to the associated feedback cycles. This means that system design seeks not just loose coupling but a decomposition that supports flow and lowers dependencies and coordination needs between stream-aligned teams. Complicated-subsystem and platform teams reduce load for stream-aligned teams, where the latter are internal customers of the former's subsystem or platform capabilities (supporting all phases of development, delivery, and operations for multiple stream teams). Enabling teams likewise serve other teams, but they are service providers, helping stream-aligned teams learn new techniques, investigate new technologies, and so forth, allowing stream-aligned teams to retain focus while growing effectiveness.

Matthew Skelton and Manuel Pais have brought their considerable experience to bear, describing what these various team forms need to be successful, but also highlighting variations in context, identifying the design implications thereof, and indicating anti-patterns to avoid. They also, with great generosity, weave in insights from and offer pointers to related work. This, along with a set of case studies, further textures the book.

Team Topologies informs and enriches our understanding of organizational architecture, via the nuanced presentation of these key structural patterns, interaction modes or dynamics, and considerations for evolution. And, due to its clarity and focus, it serves as a pragmatic guide whether forming teams and enabling them to meet their challenges or helping existing teams become more effective at responsive value delivery.

—**Ruth Malan**, Architecture Consultant at
Bredemeyer Consulting

PREFACE

[Modern] organisational design...is about designing for collaborative technologies, for the voice of the customer.
—**Naomi Stanford**, *Guide to Organization Design*

Teams are always works in progress, but they are also your best shot at delivering value continuously and sustainably by aligning them with the business. Ideally, teams should be long lived and autonomous, with engaged team members. However, teams don't live in isolation. They need to understand how and when to interact with each other. And these team interactions need to evolve over time to support the distinct phases of discovery and execution that products and technology go through during their lifetimes. In short, organizations not only need to strive for autonomous teams, they also need to continuously think about and evolve themselves in order to deliver value quickly to customers.

This book offers a practical, step-by-step, adaptive model for organizational design that we have used and seen work across businesses at varying levels of maturity: Team Topologies.

However, Team Topologies is not a universal formula for building and running software systems successfully. There are teams and organizations who succeed with organizational dynamics very different from those described and recommended here (particularly in organizations with excellent culture and best practices already in place).

Team Topologies *is* meant to provide clear patterns that are straightforward for many different teams and organizations to follow and interpret, not to dictate to outstanding players how to perform. We like to think of Team Topologies as a set of music parts for an orchestra or big band, not the melody for a top jazz trumpeter. Printed music for a large musical ensemble helps the group to succeed but does not dictate every aspect of performance; lots of detail is left for the ensemble to interpret to suit the occasion, venue, or mix of players. Likewise, there is huge value in agreeing to a coherent vocabulary and way of working together across teams to achieve good software delivery.

The Team Topologies approach helps organizations that are struggling to find a way to optimize their team structure, or for those that are not yet aware of the impact team design can have on good business outcomes and software systems in particular. Team Topologies helps organizations succeed more quickly and more continuously than before.

This book is for anyone who cares about the effectiveness of the delivery and operations of software systems: C-level leaders (including CTOs/CIOs, CEOs, CFOs, and so on) managers, heads of department, software architects and systems architects, and anyone else involved in building or running software systems who wants or needs to make the delivery and running of those systems more effective.

How We Came to Write This Book

In 2013, while introducing DevOps and Continuous Delivery at a company in the UK, Matthew devised the original DevOps Topologies patterns (and anti-patterns) in a blog post titled "What Team Structure Is Right for DevOps to Flourish?"[1] At the time, the company he was consulting with was struggling to adopt modern approaches to software delivery, and the early topology patterns Matthew created provided the company a way to explore different options.

Manuel interviewed Matthew at the QCon London software development conference back in 2015, where Matthew was speaking on Conway's law and the early DevOps Topology patterns. The resulting article, "How Different Team Topologies Influence DevOps Culture," was published by *InfoQ* and translated into several languages.[2] Later that year, Manuel helped to expand the DevOps Topology patterns and there were contributions from the community.

Since then, the use of DevOps Topology patterns has exploded. They have been referenced over and over again in talks, articles, and conversations. They have helped organizations of all sizes and from varying industries around the world to think about the relationships between teams and how their interactions influence both organizational culture and software architecture.

Over time, we realized that the original DevOps Topologies presented a static view of team interrelationships that, while useful for initial discussions, was quite limited in scope. Through our combined experience with training and consulting organizations from across the world, we discovered that some teams work better relatively isolated or autonomous, while other teams work better with strong collaboration. We asked ourselves why, and we kept evolving our ideas based on feedback from our clients.

Eventually, this led to the Team Topologies as you see them presented in this book: a dynamic and evolving approach to organizational design based on real scenarios from across different geographies and industries.

How to Use This Book

Team Topologies is meant to be a functional book. It is our intention to provide content that is interactive and delivers as much learning as we are able to fit within these pages. To help with that, we have made some design choices that will help you navigate this book.

First, the book is organized in three parts:

Part I of the book explores Conway's law, the way organizational interrelationships constrain the design of systems we build, and how we can use this tendency to our advantage. We then define what we mean by teams and look at some practical constraints that affect effective teamwork.

In Part II, we investigate a set of static team patterns that have been proven in the industry and the implications of choosing one pattern over another with Conway's law and organizational context in mind. This section should help you think about team topologies that are broadly suitable for your organizational context. This part also provides some guidance in deciding how to align teams to areas of the system, taking into account Conway's law and fundamental team topologies.

Finally, in Part III, we deal with ways to evolve the organization design to provide powerful capabilities for innovation and rapid delivery in response to a quickly changing operating context. We explain how to use the Team Topologies approach to create a sensing organization that responds to the market and user demands, and accounts for the implications this has for hiring and skills.

Each part opens with a breakdown of key takeaways from each of the chapters. Throughout the chapters, we have included figures and callouts to highlight information we think is helpful to know and/or reference. We also provide easy-to-recognize scenarios, case studies, and explicit recommendations for different situations along the way.

Finally, the shapes, colors, and patterns found within many of the figures also have consistent meaning throughout much of the book. Here is the key:

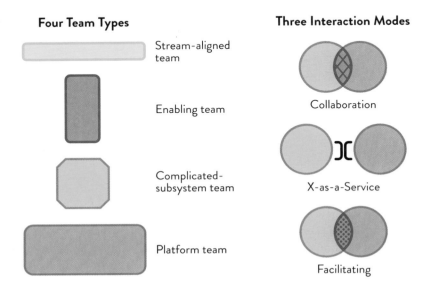

Figure 0.1: The Four Team Types and Three Interaction Modes

For the fullest understanding, you should read the book from cover to cover, as the subject matter builds up chapter by chapter. However, we have written the material so that each section is fairly independent.

In that spirit, here are some scenarios with corresponding ways to read the book that might match with your current situation:

- I need more clarity about different team types and which team types are effective.
    - Review Chapter 1 (overview), then Chapter 4 (static topologies), then Chapter 5 (fundamental topologies).
- I need to split up a large, monolithic software system.
    - Review Chapter 6 (boundaries) and then Chapter 3 (the team).
- I need to improve the architecture of the software system.

- Review Chapter 2 (Conway's law), then Chapter 4 (static topologies), then Chapter 6 (boundaries).
- I need to improve the effectiveness of software development teams.
  - Review Chapter 3 (the team), then Chapter 6 (boundaries), then Chapter 5 (fundamental topologies).
- I need to improve morale and effectiveness within teams.
  - Review Chapter 3 (the team) and then Chapter 5 (fundamental topologies).
- I need to understand where to invest effort to help with projected growth.
  - Review Chapter 1 (overview), then Chapter 5 (fundamental topologies), then Chapter 8 (topology evolution).
- I need to understand how to evolve team topologies to meet changing business needs.
  - Review Chapter 7 (dynamic aspects) and then Chapter 8 (topology evolution and organizational sensing).

Key Influences that Informed this Book

In addition to our own experience, this book is strongly influenced by several related approaches and sets of thinking. First, we assume that an organization is a sociotechnical system or ecosystem that is shaped by the interaction of individuals and the teams within it; in other words, that an organization is the interaction between people and technology. In this aspect, the book fits with ideas from the fields of: cybernetics (especially the use of the organization as a "sensing mechanism," which goes back as far as 1948, when Norbert Wiener's book *Cybernetics: Or Control and Communication in the Animal and the Machine* was first published), systems thinking (particularly the work of W. Edwards Deming), and approaches such as the Cynefin framework for assessing domain complexity (described by Dave Snowden and Mary Boone in their 2007 *Harvard Business Review* paper titled "A Leader's Framework for Decision Making"), and adaptive structuration theory (a term coined by Gerardine DeSanctis and Marshall Scott Poole in their *Organization Science* article, "Capturing the Complexity in Advanced Technology Use: Adaptive Structuration Theory," where they emphasized that the impact of technology is not a given, as it depends on how groups and organizations perceive it).

Second, we assume that "the team" is something that behaves differently from a mere collection of individuals, and that the team should be nurtured and supported in its evolution and operation. In this respect, we draw on ideas from Bruce Tuckman (who proposed the four-stages model—forming, storming, norming, performing—for team development in his 1965 paper "Developmental Sequence in Small Groups"), Russ Forrester and Allan Drexler (who explored team-based organization performance in their 1999 paper "A Model for Team-Based Organization Performance"), Pamela Knight (who found evidence that storming takes place throughout the entire lifetime of a team in her 2007 paper "Acquisition Community Team Dynamics: The Tuckman Model vs. the DAU Model"), Patrick Lencioni (who explores common interaction issues in his seminal book *The Five Dysfunctions of a Team: A Leadership Fable*), and similar team-focused theories and research.

Third, we assume that Conway's law (or a variant of it) is a strong driver of software product shape and that organizations would benefit from explicitly addressing the implications of this law. In this regard, we draw on writing and ideas from Mel Conway; from software architecture consultant and team organization design award-winner Ruth Malan; from ThoughtWorks technical director and one of the "reverse Conway maneuver" proponents James Lewis; and from similar authors and practitioners.

Finally, we draw on numerous sources that describe practical successes developing and running software systems at scale, including organizations such as Adidas, Auto Trader, Ericsson, Netflix, Spotify, TransUnion, and others. The size and speed of these organizations has made it possible for them to see tangible gains from changes in organization structure and team interaction over the space of several months to a few years.

As you travel through this book, we hope you get inspired to challenge how you think about teams, their structures, and how they function.

PART I

Teams As the Means of Delivery

KEY TAKEAWAYS

CHAPTER 1
- Conway's law suggests major gains from designing software architectures and team interactions together, since they are similar forces.
- Team Topologies clarifies team purpose and responsibilities, increasing the effectiveness of their interrelationships.
- Team Topologies takes a humanistic approach to building software systems while setting up organizations for strategic adaptability.

CHAPTER 2
- Organizations are constrained to produce designs that reflect communication paths.
- The design of the organization constrains the "solution search space," limiting possible software designs.
- Requiring everyone to communicate with everyone else is a recipe for a mess.
- Choose software architectures that encourage team-scoped flow.
- Limiting communication paths to well-defined team interactions produces modular, decoupled systems.

CHAPTER 3
- The team is the most effective means of software delivery, not individuals.
- Limit the size of multi-team groupings within the organization based on Dunbar's number.
- Restrict team responsibilities to match the maximum team cognitive load.
- Establish clear boundaries of responsibility for teams.
- Change the team working environment to help teams succeed.

The Problem with Org Charts

> Organizations should be viewed as complex and adaptive organisms rather than mechanistic and linear systems.
> —**Naomi Stanford**, Guide to Organisation Design

Technology workers are in a constant state of action: creating and updating systems at an unbelievable rate, and combining different types of technology to create a compelling user experience. Mobile applications; cloud-based services; web applications; and embedded, wearable, or industrial IoT devices all need to interoperate effectively to achieve the desired business outcomes.

Today, these systems affect nearly every aspect of people's day-to-day lives in ways that are increasingly profound. If software is poorly designed—or more importantly, if there is a mismatch in the interaction of the software, the provider, and the customer—people will be adversely affected. They can be stranded long distances from home if a taxi-hailing application fails. They may be unable to pay rent if the software or processes for internet banking fail. They may even see their life in danger if a medical device fails. Never before has explicit sociotechnical design been so important.

Building and running these highly complex, interconnected software systems is a team activity, requiring the combined efforts of people with different skills across different platforms. In addition, modern IT organizations must deliver and operate software systems rapidly *and* safely, while simultaneously growing and adapting to changes and pressures in the business or regulatory environment. Businesses can no longer choose between optimizing for stability and optimizing for speed.

But despite these risks and demands, many organizations are still organizing their people and teams in ways that are counterproductive to modern software development and operations. Organizations that rely too heavily on org charts and matrixes to split and control work often fail to create the necessary conditions to embrace innovation while still delivering at a fast pace. In order to succeed at that, organizations need stable teams and effective team patterns and interactions. They need to invest in empowered, skilled teams as the foundation for agility and adaptability. To stay alive in ever more competitive markets, organizations need teams and people who are able to sense when context changes and evolve accordingly.

The good news is that it *is* possible to be fast and safe with the right mindset and with tools that emphasize adaptability as well as repeatability, while putting teams and people at the center. As Mark Schwartz and co-authors put it in their 2016 paper *Thinking Environments*, "the organizational structure must coordinate accountabilities to support the goals of delivering high-quality, impactful software."[1]

As members of the technology teams managing these interfaces, we must shift our thinking from treating teams as collections of interchangeable individuals that will succeed as long as they follow the "right" process and use the "right" tools, to treating people and technology as a single human/computer carbon/silicon sociotechnical ecosystem. At the same time, we need to ensure that teams are intrinsically motivated and are given a real chance of doing their best work within such a system.

This chapter will introduce Team Topologies as an adaptive model for technology organization design allowing businesses to achieve speed *and* stability. But first, let's look at how real communication structures in most organizations are often quite distinct from what the org chart tells us, and what the implications of that are.

Communication Structures of an Organization

Most organizations want or are required to have a single view of their teams and people called the "org chart." This chart depicts the teams, departments, units, and other organizational entities, as well as how they relate to each other. It usually shows hierarchical lines of reporting, which imply lines of communication running "up and down" the organization.

The org chart does have its uses in the context of building software systems, specifically around regulatory and legal compliance. However, in a highly collaborative context filled with uncertainty over outcomes, relying on the org chart as a principal mechanism of splitting the work to be done leads to unrealistic expectations. We need to rely instead on decoupled, long-lived teams that can collaborate effectively to meet the challenge of balancing speed and safety.

The problem with taking the org chart at face value is that we end up trying to architect people as if they were software, neatly keeping their communication within the accepted lines. But people don't restrict their communications only to those connected lines on the chart. We reach out to whomever we depend on to get work done. We bend the rules when required to achieve our goals. That's why *actual* communication lines look quite different from the org chart, as shown in Figure 1.1 (see page 6).

CHAPTER ONE

Org Chart Thinking Is the Problem

Traditional org charts don't help us understand what the actual patterns of communication in our organization are, as illustrated in Figure 1.1. Instead, organizations need to develop more realistic pictures of the expected and actual communication happening between individuals and teams. The gaps will help inform what types of systems are a better fit for the organization.

Furthermore, decisions based on org-chart structure tend to optimize for only part of the organization, ignoring upstream and downstream effects. Local optimizations help the teams directly involved, but they don't necessarily help improve the overall delivery of value to customers. Their impact might be negligent if there are larger bottlenecks in the stream of work. For example, having teams adopting cloud and infrastructure-as-code can reduce the time to provision new infrastructure from weeks or months to minutes or hours. But if every change requires deployment (to production) approval from a board that meets once a week, then delivery speed will remain weekly at best.

Systems thinking focuses on optimizing for the whole, looking at the overall flow of work, identifying what the largest bottleneck is today, and eliminating it. Then repeat. Team Topologies focuses on how to set up dynamic team structures and interaction modes that can help teams adapt quickly to new conditions, and achieve fast and safe software delivery. This might not be your largest bottleneck today, but eventually, you will face the issue of rigid team structures with poor communication and/or inadequate processes, slowing down delivery.

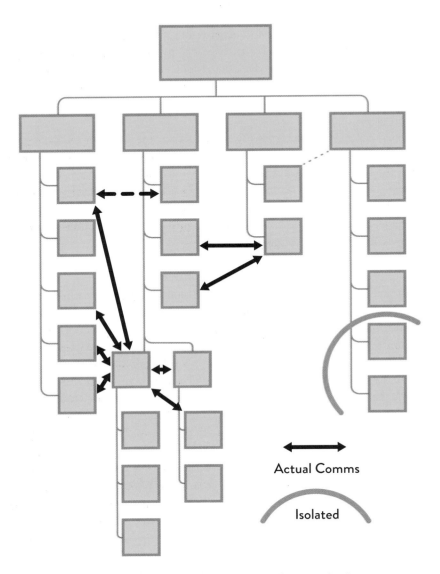

Actual Comms

Isolated

Figure 1.1: Org Chart with Actual Lines of Communication
In practice, people communicate laterally or "horizontally" with people from
other reporting lines in order to get work done. This creativity and problem solving
needs to be nurtured for the benefit of the organization, not restricted to optimize
for top-down/bottom-up communication and reporting.

Thinking of the org chart as a faithful representation of how work gets done and how teams interact with each other leads to ineffective decisions around allocation of work and responsibilities. Much like a software architecture document gets outdated as soon as the actual software development starts, an org chart is always out of sync with reality.

Naturally, we are by no means the first to acknowledge the imbalance between formal organization structures and the way work actually gets done. Geary Rummler and Alan Brache's book *Improving Performance: How to Manage the White Space on the Organization Chart* set the stage for continuous business process improvement and management. The recent focus (at least within IT) on product and team centricity, as illustrated by Mik Kersten's book on moving from *Project to Product*, is another major milestone. We like to think that Team Topologies is another piece of this puzzle—in particular, having clear and fluid team structures, responsibilities, and interaction modes.

Beyond the Org Chart

So if org charts are not an accurate representation of organizational structures, what is? Niels Pflaeging, author of *Organize for Complexity*, identifies not one but three different organizational structures in every organization:[2]

1. Formal structure (the org chart)—facilitates compliance
2. Informal structure—the "realm of influence" between individuals
3. Value creation structure—how work actually gets done based on inter-personal and inter-team reputation

Pflaeging suggests that the key to successful knowledge work organizations is in the interactions between the informal structure and the value creation structure (that is, the interactions between people and teams).[3] Other authors have proposed similar characterizations, such as Frédéric Laloux in *Reinventing Organizations* or Brian Robertson's *Holacracy* approach.[4]

The Team Topologies approach acknowledges the importance of informal and value creation structures as defined by Pflaeging. By empowering teams, and treating them as fundamental building blocks, individuals inside those teams move closer together to act as a team rather than just a group of people. On the other hand, by explicitly agreeing on interaction modes with other teams, expectations on behaviors become clearer and inter-team trust grows.

Over the last several decades, there have been many new approaches to organizing businesses, but usually the new design remains a static view of the organization that does not take into consideration the real behaviors and structures that emerge after reorganization. For instance, the "matrix management" approach that started in the 1990s—and became quite popular over the next couple of decades—tried to address the inherent complexity of highly uncertain, highly skilled work by having individuals report to both business and functional managers. Despite a clearer focus on business value compared to a purely functional organization of teams, this is still a static view of the world that becomes outdated as the business and technology domains quickly evolve.

For workers, re-orgs, like introducing matrix management, can bring a lot of fear and worry. Often, it's seen as a time and effort drain that is more likely to set the business back rather than move it forward. And once the next technological or methodological revolution hits, the business undertakes yet another re-org, breaking down established forms of communication and splitting up teams that were just starting to get their mojo.

It is increasingly clear that relying on a single, static organizational structure, like the org chart or matrix management, is untenable for effective outcomes with modern software systems. Instead of a single structure, what is needed is a model that is adaptable to the current situation—one that takes into consideration how teams grow and interact with each other. Team Topologies provides the (r)evolutionary approach required to keep teams, processes, and technology aligned for all kinds of organizations.

> The Team Topologies approach adds the dynamic and sensing aspects required for technology organizations that are missing from traditional organization design.

In her excellent 2015 book, *Guide to Organisation Design: Creating High-Performing and Adaptable Enterprises*, Naomi Stanford lists five rules of thumb for designing organizations:[5]

1. Design when there is a compelling reason.
2. Develop options for deciding on a design.
3. Choose the right time to design.
4. Look for clues that things are out of alignment.
5. Stay alert to the future.

As we continue to move through this book, we will explore how to address these five heuristics for organization design.

Team Topologies: A New Way of Thinking about Teams

The Team Topologies approach brings new thinking around effective team structures for enterprise software delivery. It provides a consistent, actionable guide for evolving team design to continuously cope with technology, people, and business changes, covering size, shape, placement, responsibilities, boundaries, and interaction of teams building and running modern software systems.

Team Topologies provides four fundamental team types—*stream-aligned*, *platform, enabling*, and *complicated-subsystem*—and three core team interaction modes—*collaboration, X-as-a-Service*, and *facilitating*. Together with awareness of Conway's law, team cognitive load, and how to become a sensing organization, Team Topologies results in an effective and humanistic approach to building and running software systems.

In particular, it looks at ways in which different team topologies can evolve with technological and organizational maturity. Periods of technical and product discovery typically require a highly collaborative environment (with overlapping team boundaries) to succeed. But keeping the same structures when discovery is over (established technologies and product) can lead to wasted effort and misunderstandings.

By emphasizing an adaptive model for organization design and actively prioritizing the interrelationship of teams, the Team Topologies approach provides a key technology-agnostic mechanism for modern software-intensive enterprises to sense when a change in strategy is required (either from a business or technology viewpoint). The end goal is to help teams produce software that aligns with customer needs and is easier to build, run, and own.

Team Topologies also emphasizes a humanistic approach to designing and building software systems. It sees the team as an indivisible element of software delivery and acknowledges that teams have a finite cognitive capacity that needs to be respected. Together with the dynamic team design solidly grounded on Conway's law, Team Topologies becomes a strategic tool for solution discovery.

The Revival of Conway's Law

We've mentioned the importance of Conway's law as a driver for team design and evolution. But what is this law exactly?

In 1968, the computer systems researcher Mel Conway published a paper in *Datamation* called "How Do Committees Invent?" in which he explored the relationship between organizational structure and the resulting design of systems. The article is full of sparkling insights, some of which we cover later in this chapter, but this is the phrase that became known as *Conway's law*: "Organizations which design systems...are constrained to produce designs which are copies of the communication structures of these organizations."[6]

Conway based his observation on organizations building early electronic computer systems. In his words, this "law" indicates the strong correlation between an organization's real communication paths (the value creation structures mentioned by Pflaeging) and the resulting software architecture,[7] or what author Allan Kelly calls the "homomorphic force."[8] This homomorphic force tends to make things the same shape between the software architecture and team structures. In other words, building software requires an understanding of communication across teams in order to realistically consider what kind of software architectures are feasible. If the desired theoretical system architecture does not fit the organizational model, then one of the two will need to change.

Eric Raymond stated this in a humorous way in his book *The New Hacker's Dictionary:* "If you have four groups working on a compiler, you'll get a 4-pass compiler."[9]

Since 1968, it has become increasingly clear that Conway's law continues to apply to all software built. Those of us who have built software systems that had to comply with an "architecture blueprint" can surely remember having times when it felt like we were fighting against the architecture rather than it helping steer our work in the right direction. Well, that's Conway's law in action.

> Team structures must match the required software architecture or risk producing unintended designs.

A sort of "revival" of Conway's law took place around 2015, when microservices architectures were on the rise. In particular, James Lewis, Technical Director at Thoughtworks, and others came up with the idea of applying an "inverse Conway maneuver" (or reverse Conway maneuver), whereby an organization focuses on organizing team structures to match the architecture they want the system to exhibit rather than expecting teams to follow a mandated architecture design.[10]

The key takeaway here is that thinking of software architecture as a standalone concept that can be designed in isolation and then implemented by any group of teams is fundamentally wrong. This gap between architecture and team structures is visible across all types of architectures, from client-server to SOA and even microservices. Specifically, that is why monoliths need to be broken down (in particular, any indivisible software part that exceeds the cognitive capacity of any one team) while keeping a team focus, a topic we will discuss in depth in Chapter 6.

Cognitive Load and Bottlenecks

When we talk about cognitive load, it's easy to understand that any one person has a limit on how much information they can hold in their brains at any given moment. The same happens for any one team by simply adding up all the team members' cognitive capacities.

However, we hardly ever discuss cognitive load when assigning responsibilities or software parts to a given team. Perhaps because it's hard to quantify both the available capacity and what the cognitive load will be. Or perhaps because the team is expected to adapt to what it's being asked to do, no questions asked.

When cognitive load isn't considered, teams are spread thin trying to cover an excessive amount of responsibilities and domains. Such a team lacks bandwidth to pursue mastery of their trade and struggles with the costs of switching contexts.

Miguel Antunes, R&D Principle Software Engineer at OutSystems, a low-code platform vendor, relayed an example of this very challenge. Their Engineering Productivity team at OutSystems was five years old. The team's mission was to help product teams run their builds efficiently, maintain infrastructure, and improve test execution. The team kept growing and took on extra responsibilities around continuous integration (CI), continuous delivery (CD), and infrastructure automation.

Victims of their own success, sprint planning for the now eight-person-strong team was a mix and match of requests across their stack of responsibilities. Prioritization was hard, and the frequent context switching even throughout a single sprint led to a dip in people's motivation. This is not surprising if we consider Dan Pink's three elements of intrinsic motivation: autonomy (quashed by constant juggling of requests and priorities from multiple teams), mastery ("jack of all trades, master of none"), and purpose (too many domains of responsibility).[11]

While the team in this industry example was providing internal services to development teams, the effect is the same for teams working on software for external customers. The number of services and components for which a product team is responsible (in other words, the demand on the team)

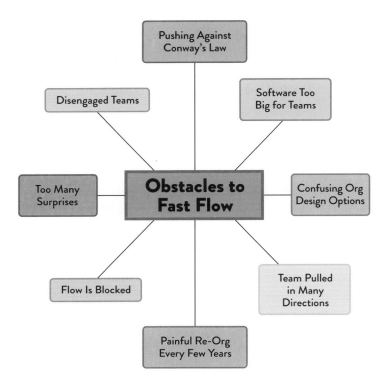

Figure 1.2: Obstacles to Fast Flow

typically keeps growing over time. However, the development of new services is often planned as if the team had full-time availability and zero cognitive load to start with. This neglect is problematic because the team is still required to fix and enhance existing services. Ultimately, the team becomes a delivery bottleneck, as their cognitive capacity has been largely exceeded, leading to delays, quality issues, and often, a decrease in team members' motivation.

We need to put the team first, advocating for restricting their cognitive loads. Explicitly thinking about cognitive load can be a powerful tool for deciding on team size, assigning responsibilities, and establishing boundaries with other teams. (We will cover this in detail in Chapter 3.)

Overall, the Team Topologies approach advocates for organization design that optimizes for *flow of change* and feedback from running systems. This requires restricting cognitive load on teams and explicitly designing the intercommunications between them to help produce the software-systems architecture that we need (based on Conway's law).

Summary: Rethink Team Structures, Purpose, and Interactions

Developing and operating software effectively for modern, interconnected systems and services requires organizations to consider many different dimensions. Historically, most organizations have seen software development as a kind of manufacturing to be completed by separate individuals arranged into functional specialties, with large projects planned up front and with little consideration for sociotechnical dynamics. This led to the prevailing problems depicted in Figure 1.2 on page 12.

The Agile, Lean IT, and DevOps movements helped demonstrate the enormous value of smaller, more autonomous teams that were aligned to the flow of business, developing and releasing in small, iterative cycles, and course correcting based on feedback from users. Lean IT and DevOps also encouraged big strides in telemetry and metrics tooling for both systems and teams, helping people building and running software to make proactive, early decisions based on past trends, rather than simply responding to incidents and problems as they arose.

However, traditional organizations have often been limited in their ability to fully reap the benefits of Agile, Lean IT, and DevOps due to their organizational models. It's no surprise that there is a strong focus on the more immediate automation and tooling adoption, while cultural and organizational changes are haphazardly addressed. The latter changes are much harder to visualize, let alone to measure their effectiveness. Yet having the right team structure, approach, and interaction in place, and understanding their need to evolve over time is a key differentiator for success in the long run.

In particular, traditional org charts are out of sync with this new reality of frequent (re)shaping of teams for collaborative knowledge work in environments filled with uncertainty and novelty. Instead, we need to take advantage of Conway's law (organizational design prevails over software architecture design), cognitive load restrictions, and a team-first approach in order to design teams with clear purposes and promote team interactions that prioritize flow of software delivery and strategic adaptability.

The goal of *Team Topologies* is to give you the approach and mental tools to enable your organization to adapt and dynamically find the places and timing when collaboration is needed, as well as when it is best to focus on execution and reduce communication overhead.

> **NOTE**
>
> We found a fascinating example of strategic and collaborative inter-action in a totally different field when researching for this book. It turns out that grouper fish and moray eels, seemingly unrelated species (silos, anyone?), explicitly collaborate (via signals) to hunt down smaller fishes that hide in crevices. The eel sneaks into the crevices and scares off smaller fish, which are then forced to come out and become easy prey for the grouper. Read on to find out how to enable the groupers and eels in your organization to join forces for better flow and business outcomes!

2 Conway's Law and Why It Matters

[Conway's law] creates an imperative to keep asking: "Is there a better design that is not available to us because of our organization?"
—**Mel Conway**, *Toward Simplifying Application Development, in a Dozen Lessons*

In Chapter 1, we discussed why organizations need to consider team organization as an integral factor to success. We also discussed the underpinning ideas and principles that help us understand how teams work within an organization. We introduced some key concepts that we will begin to build on throughout the book. In the remaining chapters of Part I, we will discuss in more detail what Conway's law reveals about teams, organization structure, and software architecture; then we will dig into what a team-first approach means. The goal in Part I is to give you the foundational principles for organization and team design that you will need to understand as you consider team topologies, starting with Conway's law.

Understanding and Using Conway's Law

Conway's law is critical to understanding the forces at play when organizing teams amidst the long-lasting, unattended impact they can have on our software systems as the latter have become larger and more interconnected than ever before. But you might wonder if a law from 1968 about software architecture has stood the test of time.

We've come a long way after all: microservices, the cloud, containers, serverless. In our experience, such novelties can help teams improve locally, but the larger the organization, the harder it becomes to reap the full benefits. The way teams are set up and interact is often based on past projects and/or legacy technologies (reflecting the latest org-chart design, which might be years old, if not decades).

If you've ever worked for a large organization, you have likely encountered examples of monolithic shared databases powering an entire business. There were, of course, valid historical reasons for the predominance of monolithic databases (such as the rise in specialism of people and teams on technical stack layers) up until DevOps and microservices gained traction. Factors such as project orientation, cost cutting via outsourcing, or junior teams without sufficient experience have contributed to the perpetuation of this (now recognizable) anti-pattern. Monolithic databases couple the applications that depend on them and become magnets for small-business logic changes at the database level (more on this in Chapter 6). Yet, to avoid them, organizations need not only good architectural practices but also actual team structures and composition that align with this new way of thinking.

Sportswear company Adidas went through an interesting transformation where they explicitly looked at Conway's law as a driver for organization design. As Fernando Cornago, Senior Director of Platform Engineering, and Markus Rautert, Vice President of Platform Engineering and Architecture, explained their IT department went from being seen as a cost center, with a single vendor providing most of the software (requiring frequent hand-offs) and only a few in-house engineers (doing more managing than engineering), to a product-oriented team organization. Adidas invested 80% of its engineering resources to creating in-house software delivery capabilities via cross-functional teams aligned with business needs. The other 20% were dedicated to a central-platform team taking care of engineering platforms and technical evolution, as well as consulting and onboarding new professionals. Adidas was able to increase release frequency of their digital products sixtyfold, while positively impacting software quality as well.[1]

Besides empirical experience, there's also an increasing body of research that generally confirms the tendencies outlined by Conway. Alan MacCormack and colleagues at Harvard Business School undertook studies of various open-source and closed-source software products and found "strong evidence to support the hypothesis that a product's architecture tends to mirror the structure of the organization in which it is developed."[2]

Studies in other industries, such as vehicle manufacturing and aircraft engine design, also corroborate this idea.[3] In fact, there has been enough industry research undertaken to show that the homomorphic force identified by Conway's law applies broadly.

This quote from Ruth Malan provides what could be seen as the modern version of Conway's law: "If the architecture of the system and the architecture of the organization are at odds, the architecture of the organization wins."[4] Malan reminds us that the organization is constrained to produce designs that match or mimic the real, on-the-ground communication structure of the organization. This has significant strategic implications for any organization designing and building software systems, whether in-house or via suppliers.

In particular, an organization that is arranged in functional silos (where teams specialize in a particular function, such as QA, DBA, or security) is unlikely to ever produce software systems that are well-architected for end-to-end flow. Similarly, an organization that is arranged primarily around sales channels for different geographic regions unlikely to produce effective software architecture that provides multiple different software services to all global regions.

Why are organizations unlikely to discover or sustain certain architectures? Conway provides some clues in his 1968 article: "Given any [particular] team organization, there is a class of design alternatives which cannot be effectively pursued by such an organization because the necessary communication paths do not exist."[5]

Communication paths (along formal reporting lines or not) within an organization effectively restrict the kinds of solutions that the organization can devise. But we can use this to our strategic advantage. If we want to discourage certain kinds of designs—perhaps those that are too focused on technical internals—we can reshape the organization to avoid this. Similarly, if we want our organization to discover and adopt certain designs—perhaps those more amenable to flow—then we can reshape the organization to help make that happen. There is, of course, no guarantee that the organization will find and use the designs we want, but at least by shaping the communication paths, we are making it more likely.

Organization design using Conway's law becomes a key strategic activity that can greatly accelerate the discovery of effective software designs and help avoid those less effective. (In Chapter 8, we go into more detail on how to evolve an organization strategically with Conway's law in mind.)

The Reverse Conway Maneuver

To increase an organization's chances of building effective software systems optimized for flow, a reverse Conway maneuver (or inverse Conway maneuver) can be undertaken to reconfigure the team intercommunications before the software is finished. Although you might get initial pushback, with sufficient willpower from management and awareness from teams this approach can and does work.

The reverse Conway maneuver gained traction in the technology world around 2015 and has been applied in many organizations since. *Accelerate: The Science of Dev Ops* by Nicole Forsgren, PhD, Jez Humble, and Gene Kim supports the importance of this strategy for high-performing organizations:

> Our research lends support to what is sometimes called the "inverse Conway maneuver," which states that organizations should evolve their team and organizational structure to achieve the desired architecture. The goal is for your architecture to support the ability of teams to get their work done—from design through to deployment—without requiring high-bandwidth communication between teams.[6]

Remember the monolithic database anti-pattern we mentioned earlier? We've seen extreme cases where, because there were no stable teams and all changes were made via temporary projects (mostly outsourced), applications became deeply coupled at the database level (shared data and procedures). This later impeded adoption of commodity systems for certain parts of the business since the latter could not be decoupled from the rest of the business logic. Instead of freeing up in-house engineers to work on differentiating features that meet evolving customer needs, accruing technical debt like this curtails an organization's ability to move faster and make a difference against competitors.

So, how can the reverse Conway maneuver help steer team organization to obtain the desired software architecture?

Let's look at a deliberate simplification of Conway's law in an organization building software to illustrate the ideas and forces at work. Let's say that four independent teams, each comprised of front-end and back-end developers, work on different parts of a system and then hand over to a database administrator (DBA) for database changes. The flow of changes may look conceptually like the diagram in Figure 2.1.

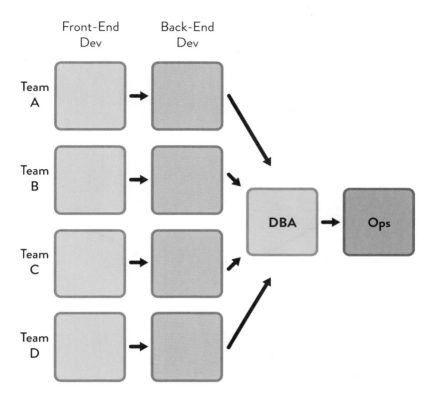

Figure 2.1: Four Teams Working on a Software System
Four separate teams consisting of front-end and back-end developers work on a
software system. Front-end devs communicate only with back-end devs, who
communicate with a single DBA for the database changes.

According to Conway's law, the software architecture that naturally emerges
from such a team design would have separate front-end and back-end components for each team, and a single, shared core database (Figure 2.2, see page 20).

In other words, the use of a shared DBA team is likely to drive the emergence
of a single shared database; and the use of separate front-end and back-end
developers is likely to drive a separation between UI and app tiers, due to the
nature of the communication taking place. If this single shared database and
four, two-tier apps is the software architecture we want, then all is well.

However, if we do *not* want a single shared database, we have a problem.
The homomorphic force identified by Conway's law is exerting a strong pull on

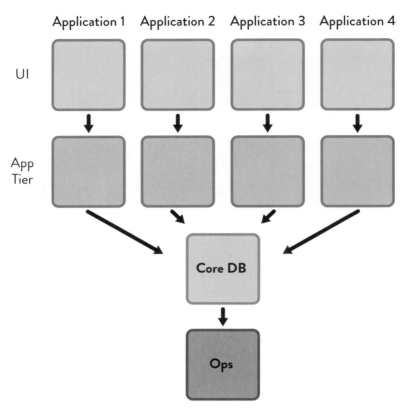

Figure 2.2: Software Architecture from Four-Team Organization
Four separate applications, each with a separate user interface (UI) and a back-
end application tier that communicate with a single shared database. This reflects
and matches the team communication architecture from Figure 2.1;
the diagram has simply been rotated ninety degrees.

the "natural" software architecture to emerge from the current organization
design and communication paths.

For example, let's say that we want to use a microservices architecture for
some new cloud-based software systems, where each separate service is independent and has its own data store (Figure 2.3, see page 21).

By applying the reverse Conway maneuver, we can design our teams to
"match" the required software architecture by having separate developers for
the client applications and the API, and a database developer within the team
rather than separate from it (Figure 2.4, see page 22).

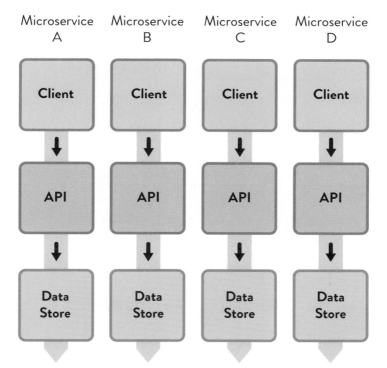

Figure 2.3: Microservices Architecture with Independent Services and Data Stores
A microservices-based architecture with four separate services, each with its own data store, API layer, and front-end client.

According to Conway's law, this team design will most "naturally" produce the desired software architecture. If we want our data store to be aligned with the business domain, then we need to avoid having a single "fan-in" database person or team (perhaps by adding a data capability within the application-development team).

Software Architectures that Encourage Team-Scoped Flow

Conway's law tells us that we need to understand what software architecture is needed *before* we organize our teams, otherwise the communication paths and incentives in the organization will end up dictating the software

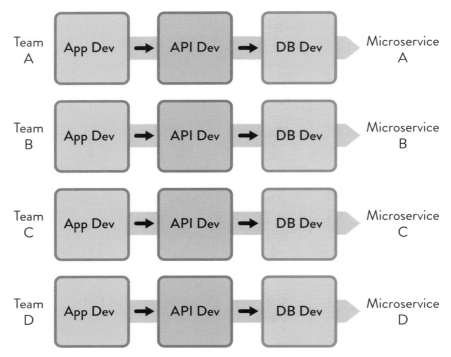

**Figure 2.4: Team Design for Microservices Architecture with
Independent Services and Data Stores**

An organization design that anticipates the homomorphic force behind Conway's
law to help produce a software architecture with four independent microservices.
(Again, this is basically the diagram in Figure 2.3 rotated ninety degrees.)

architecture. As Michael Nygard says: "Team assignments are the first draft of the architecture."[7]

For a safe, rapid flow of changes, we need to consider team-scoped flow and design the software architecture to fit it. The fundamental means of delivery is the team (see more in Chapter 3), so the system architecture needs to enable and encourage fast flow within each team. Thankfully, in practice, this means that we can follow proven software-architecture good practices:

- Loose coupling—components do not hold strong dependencies on other components
- High cohesion—components have clearly bounded responsibilities, and their internal elements are strongly related
- Clear and appropriate version compatibility

- Clear and appropriate cross-team testing

At a conceptual level, software architectures should resemble the flows of change they enable; instead of a series of interconnected components, we should be designing flows on top of an underlying platform (we will cover platforms in Chapter 5).

By keeping things team sized, we help to achieve what MacCormack and colleagues call "an 'architecture for participation' that promotes ease of understanding by limiting module size, and ease of contribution by minimizing the propagation of design changes."[8] In other words, we need a team-first software architecture that maximizes people's ability to work with it.

Keeping things decoupled and team-scoped should be a key, ongoing organization test because, as John Roberts says in *The Modern Firm*, "real gains in performance can often be achieved by adopting designs that adhere to [a] disaggregated model."[9] These performance gains are partly due to the increased rate of flow of change and partly due to the organization's ability to change the architecture to suit new contexts.

Don Reinertsen, author of *The Principles of Product Development Flow*, says "we can also exploit architecture as an enabler of rapid changes. We do this by partitioning our architecture to gracefully absorb change."[10] Architecture thus becomes an enabler, not a hindrance, but only if we take a team-first approach informed by Conway's law.

Organization Design Requires Technical Expertise

If we accept that the self-similar force (between architecture and team organization) described by Conway is real, then we also need to accept that anyone who makes decisions about the shape and placement of engineering teams is strongly influencing the software systems architecture. There is a logical implication of Conway's law here, in the words of Ruth Malan: "if we have managers deciding...which services will be built, by which teams, we implicitly have managers deciding on the system architecture."[11]

How much awareness does the HR department have about software systems? Does the group of department leaders deciding how to allocate budget across teams know of the likely effects of their choices on the viability of the software architecture?

Given that there is increasing evidence for the homomorphism behind Conway's law, it is very ineffective (perhaps irresponsible) for organizations that build software systems to decide on the shape, responsibilities, and boundaries of teams without input from technical leaders.

Organization design and software design are, in practice, two sides of the same coin, and both need to be undertaken by the same informed group of people. Allan Kelly's view of a software architect's role expands further on this idea:

> More than ever I believe that someone who claims to be an Architect needs both technical and social skills, they need to understand people and work within the social framework. They also need a remit that is broader than pure technology—they need to have a say in organizational structures and personnel issues, i.e. they need to be a manager too.[12]

Fundamentally, we need to involve technical people in organization design because they understand key software design concepts, such as APIs and interfaces, abstraction, encapsulation, and so on. Naomi Stanford puts it like this: "departments and divisions, systems, and business processes…can be designed independently as long as interfaces and boundaries with the wider organization form part of the design."[13]

Restrict Unnecessary Communication

One key implication of Conway's law is that not all communication and collaboration is good. Thus it is important to define "team interfaces" to set expectations around what kind of work requires strong collaboration and what doesn't. Many organizations assume that more communication is always better, but this is not really the case.

What we need is *focused* communication between specific teams. We need to look for unexpected communication and address the cause; as Manuel Sosa and colleagues found in their 2004 research into aircraft manufacturing, "managers should focus their efforts on understanding the causes of unaddressed design interfaces…and unpredicted team interactions…across modular systems."[14]

Mike Cohn, one of the originators of the Scrum product-development approach, asks these questions to assess the health of inter-team communication within an organization: "Does the structure minimize the number of communication paths between teams?…Does the structure encourage teams to communicate who wouldn't otherwise do so?[15]

Here, Cohn is addressing the need to ensure that if, logically, two teams shouldn't need to communicate based on the software architecture design, then something must be wrong if the teams *are* communicating. Is the API not good enough? Is the platform not suitable? Is a component missing? If we can achieve low-bandwidth communication—or even zero-bandwidth communication—between teams and still build and release software in a safe, effective, rapid way, then we should. This is visualized in Figure 2.5, which is based on Henrik Kniberg's "Real Life Agile Scaling."[16]

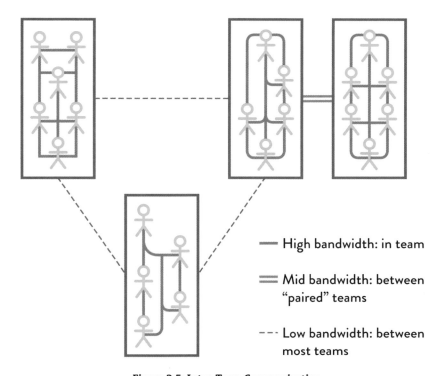

Figure 2.5: Inter-Team Communication
Communication within teams is high bandwidth. Communication between two "paired" teams can be mid bandwidth. Communication between most teams should be low bandwidth.

A simple way to restrict communication is to move two teams to different parts of the office, different floors, or even different buildings. If the teams are virtual or mostly communicate over a chat messenger tool, the volume and patterns of the team-to-team communications can help identify communications that do not match the interactions expected for the software architecture.

Similarly, if a large team regularly deals with two separate areas of the system, it can be useful to split this team into two smaller teams dedicated to each part, although only if it's the same team members who work on different systems. If the whole team works on more than one part of the system by design (for example, a newer service and an older component), keep the team together. (See Chapter 9 for more on patterns for long-term "continuity of care" for older software systems.)

Sometimes, two or more teams may feel the need to communicate on software purely because the code for their parts of the system is in the same version-control repository or is even part of the same application or service, whereas logically, it should be separate. In these cases, we need to use "fracture plane" patterns (which will be discussed in Chapter 6) to split up the software into smaller chunks that can live in separate repositories.

Everyone Does Not Need to Communicate with Everyone

With open-plan offices and, particularly, with ubiquitous, instant communication via chat tools, anyone can communicate with anyone else. In this situation, one can accidentally fall into a pattern of communication and interaction where everyone *needs to* communicate with everyone else (putting the onus on the consumer to distill what is relevant) in order to get work done. From the viewpoint of Conway's law, this will drive unintended consequences for the software systems, especially a lack of modularity between subsystems.

If the organization has an expectation that "everyone should see every message in the chat" or "everyone needs to attend the massive standup meetings" or "everyone needs to be present in meetings" to approve decisions, then we have an organization design problem. Conway's law suggests that this kind of many-to-many communication will tend to produce monolithic, tangled, highly coupled, interdependent systems that do not support fast flow. More communication is not necessarily a good thing.

Beware: Naive Uses of Conway's Law

There is a danger of misinterpreting Conway's law and creating a set of teams that appear to map well to the required architecture but, in fact, work strongly against fast flow. Furthermore, the relationship between cross-team tools and communication is often missed or ignored, but such tooling can be a powerful driver of self-similar design. In this section, we identify some potential pitfalls resulting from the naive application of Conway's law.

Tool Choices Drive Communication Patterns

The way in which teams use software communication tools can have a strong influence on communication patterns between teams. A common problem in organizations struggling to build and run modern software systems is a mismatch between the responsibility boundaries for teams or departments and those for tools. Sometimes an organization has multiple tools when a single one would suffice (providing a common, shared view). Other times, a single tool is used and problems arise because teams need separate ones.

As we've seen, Conway's law tells us that an organization is constrained to produce designs that are copies of its communication structures. We therefore need to be mindful of the effect of shared tools on the way teams interact. If we want teams to collaborate, then shared tools make sense. If we need a clear responsibility boundary between teams, then separate tools (or separate instances of the same tool) may be best.

Let's say we need a software development team to work closely with the IT operations team; having separate ticketing or incident-management tools for the two teams will likely result in poor inter-team communication. To help these teams collaborate and communicate, we should choose a tool that can meet the needs of both groups. Similarly, having a special "production only" tool that is limited to teams with security access to production should be avoided. If that tool interacts with or measures the software being built, then the restricted access to the tool is likely to drive a communication gap between teams with access and teams without. The tool can help or hinder communication flow and, therefore, the effective interaction of teams.

> **TIP**
>
> **Make information visible while keeping security in place.**
> Log-aggregation tools provide a simple solution for application teams that need to consult production logs (for debugging purposes, for instance) but do not have access to production environments. Such tools ship all the logs to an external location, where they get processed and indexed together (and anonymized if need be), making it

However, when responsibility boundaries between two teams do *not* overlap (when the teams have very distinct roles without much need to collaborate), we will not get much value from insisting on the same incident-tracking tool or even the same monitoring tool for the two teams, particularly if one of the teams is outside the organization providing a service.

In summary, don't select a single tool for the whole organization without considering team inter-relationships first. Have separate tools for independent teams, and use shared tools for collaborative teams.

Many Different Component Teams

Some organizations have naively used Conway's law to create many different component teams focused on building small parts of systems. Component teams—better called complicated-subsystem teams (see Chapter 5)—are occasionally needed but only for exceptional cases, where very detailed expertise is required. Generally speaking, we need to optimize for fast flow, so stream-aligned teams are preferred. We will cover these aspects more in Chapter 5.

Repeated Reorganizations that Create Fiefdoms or Reduce Headcount

The underlying aim of many "reorganizations" in the past was to reduce staff or create fiefdoms of power for managers and leaders. When we change the organization structure to accommodate Conway's law, we are aiming to improve the space (context, constraints, etc.) in which organizations search for solutions with software systems. These two approaches are mutually exclusive. With software and "product" companies, structure should anticipate product architecture. Combined with a team-first approach, regular reorganizations for management reasons should become a thing of the past.

To put this in the strongest way, regular reorganizations for the sake of management convenience or reducing headcount actively destroy the ability of organizations to build and operate software systems effectively. Reorganizations that ignore Conway's law, team cognitive load, and related dynamics risk acting like open heart surgery performed by a child: highly destructive.

Summary: Conway's Law Is Critical for Efficient Team Design in Tech

Conway's law tells us that an organization's structure and the actual communication paths between teams persevere in the resulting architecture of the systems built. They void the attempts of designing software as a separate activity from the design of the teams themselves.

The effects of this simple law are far reaching. On one hand, the organization's design limits the number of possible solutions for a given system's architecture. On the other hand, the speed of software delivery is strongly affected by how many team dependencies the organization design instills.

Fast flow requires restricting communication between teams. Team collaboration is important for gray areas of development, where discovery and expertise is needed to make progress. But in areas where execution prevails—not discovery—communication becomes an unnecessary overhead.

One key approach to achieving the software architecture (and associated benefits like speed of delivery or time to recover from failure) is to apply the reverse Conway maneuver: designing teams to match the desired architecture. We provided a simple example where an organization could avoid a monolithic database by embedding database skills in the application team, so that they had sufficient autonomy to maintain a separate data store (perhaps relying on a centralized DBA team for recommendations on database design or synchronization with other databases).

In short, by considering the impact of Conway's law when designing software architectures and/or reorganizing team structures, you will be able to takeadvantage of the isomorphic force at play, which converges the software architecture and the team design.

3 Team-First Thinking

> Disbanding high-performing teams is worse than vandalism: it is corporate psychopathy.
>
> —**Allan Kelly**, *Project Myopia*

Experts in organizational behavior have known for decades that modern complex systems require effective team performance: in particular, Driskell and Salas found that teams working as a cohesive unit perform far better than collections of individuals for knowledge-rich, problem-solving tasks that require high amounts of information.[1] Even previously hierarchical organizations such as the US Army have adopted the team as the fundamental unit of operation. In the bestselling book *Team of Teams*, retired US Army General Stanley McChrystal notes that the best-performing teams "accomplish remarkable feats not simply because of the individual qualifications of their members but because *those members coalesce into a single organism*."[2] (italics added)

In software development specifically, the speed, frequency, complexity, and diversity of changes needed for modern software-rich systems means that teams are essential. Relying on individuals to comprehend and effectively deal with the volume and nature of information required to build and evolve modern software is not sustainable. In fact, research by Google on their own teams found that who is on the team matters less than the team dynamics; and that when it comes to measuring performance, teams matter more than individuals.[3] We must, therefore, start with the team for effective software delivery.

There are multiple aspects to consider and nurture: team size, team lifespan, team relationships, and team cognition.

Use Small, Long-Lived Teams as the Standard

In this book, "team" has a very specific meaning. By team, we mean a stable grouping of five to nine people who work toward a shared goal as a unit. We consider the team to be the smallest entity of delivery within the organization. Therefore, an organization should never assign work to individuals; only to teams. In all aspects of software design, delivery, and operation, we start with the team.

In most organizations, an effective team has a maximum size of around seven to nine people. Amazon, for instance, is known for limiting the size of its software teams to those that can be fed by two pizzas.[4] This limit, recommended by popular frameworks such as Scrum, derives from evolutionary limits on group recognition and trust known as Dunbar's number (after anthropologist Robin Dunbar). Dunbar found fifteen to be the limit of the number of people one person can trust deeply.[5] From those, only around five people can be known and trusted closely.[6]

Allowing teams to grow beyond the magic seven-to-nine size imperils the viability of the software being built by that team, because trust will begin to break down and unsuitable decisions might ensue. Organizations need to maximize trust between people on a team, and that means limiting the number of team members.

When delivering changes rapidly, it is important to ensure that high trust is explicitly valued and designed for. High trust is what enables a team to innovate and experiment. If trust is missing or reduced due to a larger group of people, speed and safety of delivery will suffer.

> **NOTE**
>
> **High-trust organizations may sustain larger teams.**
> There are exceptions to the seven-to-nine rule, but these are rare.
> If an organization has engendered a very strong culture of trust,
> mutual respect, and acceptance of failure, teams might work at
> up to around fifteen people. However, in our experience, very few
> organizations fit this criteria.

Smaller Size Fosters Trust

The limit on team size and Dunbar's number extends to groupings of teams, departments, streams of work, lines of business, and so on. In addition to Dunbar's number, anthropological research shows that the type and depth of relationship we can have with people has clear limits:[7]

- Around five people—limit of people with whom we can hold close personal relationships and working memory
- Around fifteen people—limit of people with whom we can experience deep trust
- Around fifty people—limit of people with whom we can have mutual trust
- Around 150 people—limit of people whose capabilities we can remember

Some researchers have identified possible limits to effective social relationships at around 500 and 1,500 (there is roughly a three times multiplier at work here). The key point is that—whether we like it or not—there are natural restrictions on the size of effective groupings within any organization. As the size of a group increases, the dynamics and behaviors between group members will be subtly or radically different, and patterns and rules that worked at a smaller scale will probably fail to work at a larger scale.

Teams need trust to operate effectively, but if the size of a group grows too large for the necessary level of trust, that group can no longer be as effective as it was when it was a smaller unit. Within an organization building and running software systems, it is therefore important to consciously limit the size of team groupings to Dunbar's number to help achieve predictable behavior and interactions from those teams:

- A single team: around five to eight people (based on industry experience)
  - In high-trust organizations: no more than fifteen people
- Families ("tribes"): groupings of teams of no more than fifty people
  - In high-trust organizations: groupings of no more than 150 people
- Divisions/streams/profit & loss (P&L) lines: groupings of no more than 150 or 500 people

Organizations can be composed from Dunbar-compatible groupings of these sizes; when one of the limits is reached, the need to split off another unit as a semi-independent grouping arises. We can visualize this "scaling by Dunbar" as concentric circles of increasingly larger or smaller groups (see Figure 3.1, based on the "onion" concept from James Lewis[8]):

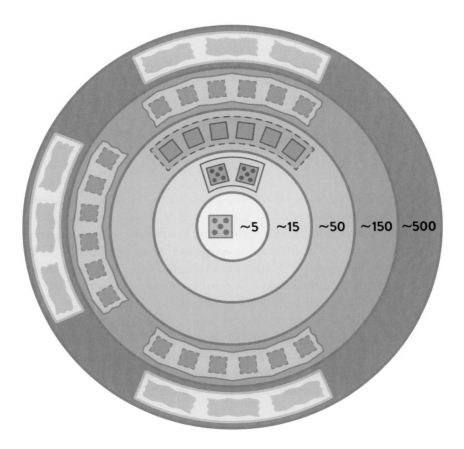

Figure 3.1: Scaling Teams Using Dunbar's Number
Organizational groupings should follow Dunbar's number, beginning with around
five people (or eight for software teams), then increasing to around fifteen people,
then fifty, then 150, then 500, and so on.

In the context of products and services enabled by software systems, the limits exposed by Dunbar's number mean that the number of people in different business lines or streams of work should also explicitly be limited when the number of people in a department exceeds fifty (or 150, or 500), the internal and external dynamics with other groupings will change. This, in turn, means that the software architecture needs to be realigned with the new team groupings so that teams can continue to own the architecture effectively. This is an example of what we like to call "team-first architecture," which requires a substantially new way of thinking for many organizations; but companies like Amazon (with its "two-pizza" rule) have proven it can be a highly successful and scalable approach.[9]

> **TIP**
>
> **Team-first software architecture is driven by Dunbar's number.**
> Expect to change the architecture of software systems to fit with the limits on human interactions set by Dunbar's number. Approaches like microservices can help if applied with a team-first perspective.

Work Flows to Long-Lived Teams

Teams take time to form and be effective. Typically, a team can take from two weeks to three months or more to become a cohesive unit. When (or if) a team reaches that special state, it can be many times more effective than individuals alone. If it takes three months for a team to become highly effective, we need to provide stability around and within the team to allow them to reach that level.

There is little value in reassigning people to different teams after a six-month project where the team has just begun to perform well. As Fred Brooks points out in his classic book *The Mythical Man-Month*, adding new people to a team doesn't immediately increase its capacity (this became known as *Brooks's law*).[10] In fact, it quite possibly reduces capacity during an initial stage. There's a ramp-up period necessary to bring people up to speed, but the communication lines inside the team also increase significantly with every new member. Not only that, but there is an emotional adaptation required both from new and old team members in order to understand and accommodate each other's points of view and work habits (the "storming" stage of Tuckman's team-development model).[11]

The best approach to team lifespans is to keep the team stable and "flow the work to the team," as Allan Kelly says in his 2018 book *Project Myopia*.[12]

Teams should be stable but not static, changing only occasionally and when necessary.

In high-trust organizations, people may change teams once a year without major detrimental effects on team performance. For example, at cloud software specialist Pivotal, "an engineer would switch teams about every 9 to 12 months."[13] In typical organizations with lower levels of trust, people should remain in the same team for longer (perhaps eighteen months or two years), and the team should be given coaching to improve and sustain team cohesion.

NOTE

Beyond the Tuckman Teal Performance Model

The Tuckman model describes how teams perform in four stages:

1. Forming: assembling for the first time
2. Storming: working through initial differences in personality and ways of working
3. Norming: evolving standard ways of working together
4. Performing: reaching a state of high effectiveness

However, in recent years, research by people like Pamela Knight has found that this model is not quite accurate, and that storming actually takes places continually throughout the life of the team.[14] Organizations should continually nurture team dynamics to maintain high performance.

The Team Owns the Software

With small, long-lived teams in place, we can begin to improve the ownership of software. Team ownership helps to provide the vital "continuity of care" that modern systems need in order to retain their operability and stay fit for purpose. Team ownership also enables a team to think in multiple "horizons"—from exploration stages to exploitation and execution—to better care for software and its viability. As Jez Humble, Joanne Molesky, and Barry O'Reilly put it in their book *Lean Enterprise*,[15] Horizon 1 covers the immediate future with products and services that will deliver results the same year; Horizon 2 covers the next few periods, with an expanding reach of the products and services; and Horizon 3 covers many months ahead, where experimentation is needed to assess market fit and suitability of new services, products, and features.

The danger of allowing multiple teams to change the same system or subsystem is that no one owns either the changes made or the resulting mess. However, when a single team owns the system or subsystem, and the team has the autonomy to plan their own work, then that team can make sensible decisions about short-term fixes with the knowledge that they will be removing any dirty fixes in the next few weeks. Awareness of and ownership over these different time horizons helps a team care for the code more effectively.

Every part of the software system needs to be owned by exactly one team. This means there should be no shared ownership of components, libraries, or code. Teams may use shared services at runtime, but every running service, application, or subsystem is owned by only one team. Outside teams may submit pull requests or suggestions for change to the owning team, but they cannot make changes themselves. The owning team may even trust another team so much that they grant them access to the code for a period of time, but only the original team retains ownership.

Note that team ownership of code should not be a territorial thing. The team takes responsibility for the code and cares for it, but individual team members should not feel like the code is theirs to the exclusion of others. Instead, teams should view themselves as stewards or caretakers as opposed to private owners. Think of code as gardening, not policing.

Team Members Need a Team-First Mindset

The team should be the fundamental means of delivery rather than the individual. If we follow this team-first approach, we need to ensure that the people *within* our teams also have (or develop) a team-first mindset. This may be unfamiliar to some people, but with the right coaching and time to learn, many people adapt.

For teams to work, team members should put the needs of the team above their own. They should:

- Arrive for stand-ups and meetings on time.
- Keep discussions and investigations on track.
- Encourage a focus on team goals.
- Help unblock other team members before starting on new work.
- Mentor new or less experienced team members.
- Avoid "winning" arguments and, instead, agree to explore options.

However, even with coaching, some people are unsuitable to work on teams or are unwilling to put team needs above their own. Such people can destroy teamwork and, in extreme cases, destroy teams. These people are "team toxic" and need to be removed before damage is done. There is a good amount of research in this area. For example, one study found that "collectively oriented team members were more likely to attend to the task inputs of other team members and to improve their performance during team interaction than egocentric team members."[16]

Embrace Diversity in Teams

In the context of rapidly changing requirements and technologies, teams must continuously find novel and creative ways to address the challenges placed upon them and to communicate effectively with other teams. Recent research in both civilian and military contexts strongly suggests that teams with members of diverse backgrounds tend to produce more creative solutions more rapidly and tend to be better at empathizing with other teams' needs.[17]

This diverse mix of people also appears to foster better results, as team members make fewer assumptions about the context and needs of their software users. Tom DeMarco and Timothy Lister, authors of the influential book *Peopleware*, observe that "a little bit of heterogeneity can be an enormous aid to create a jelled team."[18] In the context of discovering new possibilities, having a variety of viewpoints and experiences helps teams traverse the landscape of solutions much more rapidly. As Naomi Stanford, author of *Guide to Organisation Design*, puts it: "people and organizations benefit from a diverse workforce where differences spark positive energy."[19]

Reward the Whole Team, Not Individuals

W. Edwards Deming, author of *Out of the Crisis* and a pivotal figure in the Lean manufacturing movement, identified one of his key fourteen points for management as "abolishment of the annual or merit rating and of management by objective."[20] Looking to reward individual performance in modern organizations tends to drive poor results and damages staff behavior. One particularly insidious usage of individual bonuses is when companies use it to leverage their end-of-year profitability. Outstanding individual efforts might receive limited or no bonuses because of a crisis year. This increases the misalignment between the individual's merits and the bonus they actually receive, leading to frustration and demotivation.

With a team-first approach, the whole team is rewarded for their combined effort. One of the defining features of work at technology company Nokia during its hugely successful years in the 1990s and 2000s was: "Pay differences across the organization were muted. Bonuses were small and typically paid on a team basis and on overall company performance, not individually."[21]

The same can be applied to training budgets. With a team-first approach, the whole team rather than each individual gets a single training budget. If the team wants to send the same person to six or seven conferences during the year because they are so good at reporting back to the team, that should be the team's decision.

Good Boundaries Minimize Cognitive Load

Having established the team as the fundamental means of delivery, organizations also need to ensure that the cognitive load on a team is not too high. A team working with software systems that require too high of a cognitive load cannot effectively own or safely evolve the software. In this section, we will identify ways in which the cognitive load on teams can be detected and limited in order to safely promote fast flow of change.

Restrict Team Responsibilities to Match Team Cognitive Load

One of the least acknowledged factors that increases friction in modern software delivery is the ever-increasing size and complexity of codebases that teams have to work with. This creates an unbounded cognitive load on teams.

Cognitive load also applies to teams that do less coding and more execution of tasks, like a traditional operations or infrastructure team. They can also suffer from excessive cognitive load in terms of domains of responsibility, number of applications they need to operate, and tools they need to manage.

With a team-first approach, the team's responsibilities are matched to the cognitive load that the team can handle. The positive ripple effect of this can change how teams are designed and how they interact with each other across an organization.

For software-delivery teams, a team-first approach to cognitive load means limiting the size of the software system that a team is expected to work with; that is, organizations should not allow a software subsystem to grow beyond the cognitive load of the team responsible for the software. This has strong and quite radical implications for the shape and architecture of software systems, as we shall see later in the book.

Cognitive load was characterized in 1988 by psychologist John Sweller as "the total amount of mental effort being used in the working memory."[22] Sweller defines three different kinds of cognitive load:

- Intrinsic cognitive load—relates to aspects of the task fundamental to the problem space (e.g., "What is the structure of a Java class?" "How do I create a new method?")
- Extraneous cognitive load—relates to the environment in which the task is being done (e.g., "How do I deploy this component again?" "How do I configure this service?")
- Germane cognitive load—relates to aspects of the task that need special attention for learning or high performance (e.g., "How should this service interact with the ABC service?")

For example, the *intrinsic cognitive load* for a web application developer could be the knowledge of the computer language being used (on top of the fundamentals of programming), the *extraneous cognitive load* might be details of the commands needed to instantiate a dynamic testing environment (which needs multiple hard-to-remember console commands), and the *germane cognitive load* could be the specific aspects of the business domain that the application developer is programming (such as an invoicing system or a video-processing algorithm). Jo Pearce's work on cognitive load in the context of software development provides numerous additional examples.[23]

Broadly speaking, for effective delivery and operations of modern software systems, organizations should attempt to minimize intrinsic cognitive load (through training, good choice of technologies, hiring, pair programming, etc.) and eliminate extraneous cognitive load altogether (boring or superfluous tasks or commands that add little value to retain in the working memory and can often be automated away), leaving more space for germane cognitive load (which is where the "value add" thinking lies).

As we have seen earlier in this chapter, there is an effective maximum size of seven to nine members for a team building and running software systems (see Figure 3.1 on page 34), so it follows that there is a maximum amount of cognitive load that a certain team can deal with. Many organizations do not consider the cognitive load on teams when assigning responsibility for parts of a software system, instead assuming that by adding more teams to the problem, the cognitive load will be shared across the teams. Instead, the teams will suffer from similar communication and interaction strains as mentioned in Brooks's law.

If we stress the team by giving it responsibility for part of the system that is beyond its cognitive load capacity, it ceases to act like a high-performing unit and starts to behave like a loosely associated group of individuals, each trying to accomplish their individual tasks without the space to consider if those are in the team's best interest.

Limiting the cognitive load for a team means limiting the size of the subsystem or area on which the team works, a tactic suggested by Driskell and colleagues in their research paper: "For those settings in which effective teamwork is critical, it may be necessary to structure the task to make it less demanding (i.e., by delegating subtasks), so that attention can be maintained on essential task and teamwork cues.[24]

At the same time, the team needs the space to continuously try to reduce the amount of intrinsic and extraneous load they currently have to deal with (via training, practice, automation, and any other useful techniques).

Measure the Cognitive Load Using Relative Domain Complexity

A simple and quick way to assess cognitive load is to ask the team, in a non-judgmental way: "Do you feel like you're effective and able to respond in a timely fashion to the work you are asked to do?"

While not an accurate measure, the answer will help gauge whether teams are feeling overloaded. If the answer is clearly negative, organizations can apply some heuristics to understand if and why cognitive load is too high. If it is, the organization needs to take the necessary steps to reduce cognitive load, thus ensuring that the team is able to be effective and proactive again. Incidentally, this will increase motivational levels within the team as members see more value and purpose in their work.

Trying to determine the cognitive load of software using simple measures such as lines of code, number of modules, classes, or methods is misguided. Computer researcher Graylin Jay and colleagues found in 2009 that some programming languages are more verbose than others (and after the emergence of microservices, polyglot systems became increasingly more common), and teams using more abstractions and reusing code will have smaller but not necessarily simpler codebases.[25]

When measuring cognitive load, what we really care about is the domain complexity—how complex is the problem that we're trying to solve with software? A domain is a more largely applicable concept than software size. For example, running and evolving a toolchain to support continuous delivery typically requires a fair amount of tool integration and testing. Some automation code will be needed, but orders of magnitude less than the code needed for building a customer-facing application. Domains help us think across the board and use common heuristics.

While there is no formula for cognitive load, we can assess the number and relative complexity (internal to the organization) of domains for which a given team is responsible. The Engineering Productivity team at OutSystems that we mentioned in Chapter 1 realized that the different domains they were responsible for (build and continuous integration, continuous delivery, test automation, and infrastructure automation) had caused them to become overloaded. The team was constantly faced with too much work and context switching prevailed, with tasks coming in from different product areas simultaneously. There was a general sense in the team that they lacked sufficient domain knowledge, but they had no time to invest in acquiring it. In fact, most of their cognitive load was extraneous, leaving very little capacity for value-add intrinsic or germane cognitive load.

The team made a bold decision to split into microteams, each responsible for a single domain/product area: IDE productivity, platform-server productivity, and infrastructure automation. The two productivity microteams were aligned (and colocated) with the respective product areas (IDE and platform server). Changes that overlapped domains were infrequent; therefore, the previous single-team model was optimizing for the exceptions rather than the rule. With the new structure, the teams collaborated closely (even creating temporary microteams when necessary) on cross-domain issues that required a period of solution discovery but not as a permanent structure.

After only a few months, the results were above their best expectations. Motivation went up as each microteam could now focus on mastering a single domain (plus they didn't have a lead anymore, empowering team decisions). The mission for each team was clear, with less context switching and frequent intra-team communication (thanks to a single shared purpose rather than a collection of purposes). Overall, the flow and quality of the work (in terms of fitness of the solutions for product teams) increased significantly.

Limit the Number and Type of Domains per Team

To be clear, there is no final answer for "Is this the right number and type of domain for this team?" Domains are not static and neither is the team's cognitive capacity. But the reasoning around relative domain complexity can help shape teams' responsibilities and boundaries. When in doubt about the complexity of a domain, always prioritize how the responsible team feels about it. Downplaying the complexity (e.g., "There are plenty of tools for continuous delivery—it's not difficult.") in order to "fit in" more domains with a single team will only lead to failure.

To get started, identify distinct domains that each team has to deal with, and classify these domains into simple (most of the work has a clear path of action), complicated (changes need to be analyzed and might require a few iterations on the solution to get it right), or complex (solutions require a lot of experimentation and discovery). You should finetune the resulting classification by comparing pairs of domains across teams: How does domain A stack against domain B? Do they have similar complexity or is one clearly more complex than the other? Does the current domain classification reflect that?

The first heuristic is to assign each domain to a single team. If a domain is too large for a team, instead of splitting responsibilities of a single domain to multiple teams, first split the domain into subdomains and then assign each new subdomain to a single team. (See Chapter 6 for more help on how to break down large domains.)

The second heuristic is that a single team (considering the golden seven-to-nine team size) should be able to accommodate two to three "simple" domains. Because such domains are quite procedural, the cost of context switching between domains is more bearable, as responses are more mechanical. In this context, a simple domain for a team might be an older software system that has only minor, occasional, straightforward changes. However, there is a risk here of diminishing team members' motivation due to the more routine nature of their work.

The third heuristic is that a team responsible for a complex domain should not have any more domains assigned to them—not even a simple one. This is due to the cost of disrupting the flow of work (solving complex problems takes time and focus) and prioritization (there will be a tendency to resolve the simple, predictable problems as soon as they come in, causing further delays in the resolution of complex problems, which are often the most important for the business).

The last heuristic is to avoid a single team responsible for two complicated domains. This might seem feasible with a larger team of eight or nine people, but in practice, the team will behave as two subteams (one for each domain), yet everyone will be expected to know about both domains, which increases cognitive load and cost of coordination. Instead, it's best to split the team into two separate teams of five people (by recruiting one or two more team members), so they can each be more focused and autonomous. (See Figure 3.2 on page 44.)

As always, these are only recommendations, not a definitive path to success. Use these guidelines as a starting point from which to adapt as your

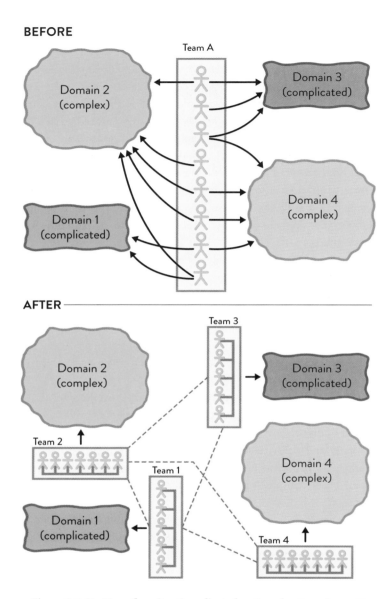

BEFORE

AFTER

Figure 3.2: No More than One Complicated or Complex Domain per Team

Before: a larger team is spread thin across four domains (two complicated and two complex) and struggles to perform well. Intra-team morale is negatively affected, with frequent context switches and individual disengagement. After: with multiple smaller teams each focusing on a single domain, motivation rises and the team delivers faster and more predictably. Low bandwidth inter-team collaboration allows solving occasional issues affecting two or more domains.

organization evolves and learns. Always remember that, in the end, even if the allocation of domains seems to make sense, if the teams doing the work are still feeling overwhelmed, stress builds up and morale weakens, leading to poor results.

Match Software Boundary Size to Team Cognitive Load

To keep software delivery teams effective and able to own and evolve parts of the software systems, we need to take a team-first approach to the size of software subsystems and the placement of boundaries. Instead of designing a

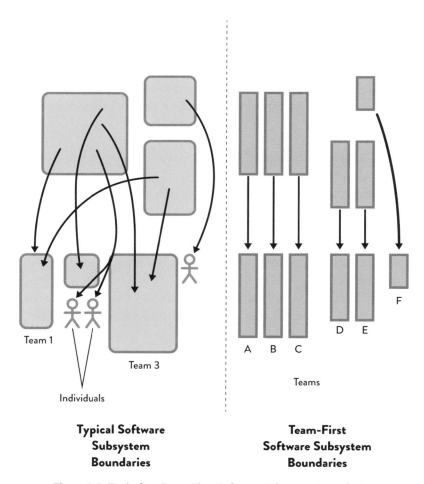

Typical Software Subsystem Boundaries

Team-First Software Subsystem Boundaries

Figure 3.3: Typical vs. Team-First Software Subsystem Boundaries

system in the abstract, we need to design the system and its software boundaries to fit the available cognitive load within delivery teams.

Instead of choosing between a monolithic architecture or a microservices architecture, design the software to fit the maximum team cognitive load. Only then can we hope to achieve sustainable, safe, rapid software delivery. This team-first approach to software boundaries leads to favoring certain styles of software architecture, such as small, decoupled services. We can visualize this team-first approach to software subsystem boundaries in Figure 3.3 (see page 45).

On the left, we see typical software subsystem boundaries, with different parts of systems or products assigned to a mix of multiple teams, single teams, and individuals. On the right, we see the Team Topologies' team-first approach to software subsystem boundaries, with every part of the system being team sized and owned by one team.

To increase the size of a software subsystem or domain for which a team is responsible, tune the ecosystem in which the team works in order to maximize the cognitive capacity of the team (by reducing the intrinsic and extraneous types of load):

- Provide a team-first working environment (physical or virtual). (You'll see more later in this chapter).
- Minimize team distractions during the workweek by limiting meetings, reducing emails, assigning a dedicated team or person to support queries, and so forth.
- Change the management style by communicating goals and outcomes rather than obsessing over the "how," what McChrystal calls "Eyes On, Hands Off" in *Team of Teams*.[26]
- Increase the quality of developer experience (DevEx) for other teams using your team's code and APIs through good documentation, consistency, good UX, and other DevEx practices.
- Use a platform that is explicitly designed to reduce cognitive load for teams building software on top of it.

By actively reducing extraneous mental overheads for teams and team members through these and similar approaches, organizations can give teams more cognitive space to take on more challenging parts of the software systems. Conversely, if an organization does not have team-first office space, good management practices, and especially a team-first platform, then the size of software subsystems that teams can take on will be smaller. A larger number of smaller parts requires more teams to work on them, costing more. Taking a team-first approach to software subsystem boundaries by designing for cognitive load means happier teams and (eventually) lower costs.

Albert Bertilsson, Solution Team Lead, and Gustaf Nilsson Kotte, Web Developer, felt the weight of a continuously increasing cognitive load on the mobile team they were leading at IKEA back in 2017. As they relayed to us, in the previous year, the team kept growing as a result of successful delivery of multiple projects in a short period of time and across multiple markets.

This high-performing team kept adding more and more responsibilities on their shoulders, as the number of software products they maintained kept increasing. Eventually, they started to run into problems due to some work streams preventing the releases of others. Despite understandable pushback from the team, Bertilsson and Kotte managed to convince team members that they really had two products in the same codebase and needed to split the team in two, following Conway's law. An interesting bit to retain here is that this was a high-performing team with all the intrinsic motivators (autonomy, mastery, and purpose), yet they were still feeling the pains of cognitive overload.

A further benefit of taking a team-first approach to software boundaries is that the team tends to easily develop a shared mental model of the software being worked on. Research has shown that the similarity of team mental models is a good predictor of team performance, meaning fewer mistakes, more coherent code, and more rapid delivery of outcomes.[27] As we begin to optimize more and more for the team, the benefits begin to compound in a positive way.

> **TIP**
>
> "Minimize cognitive load for others" is one of the most useful heuristics for good software development.

Design "Team APIs" and Facilitate Team Interactions

Now that we see the team as the fundamental means of delivery, we can begin to design other things around the team. In this section, we explore concepts such as the team API and well-defined team interactions as ways to produce a coherent, dynamic network of cleanly communicating teams.

Define "Team APIs" that Include Code, Documentation, and User Experience

With stable, long-lived teams that own specific bits of the software systems, we can begin to build a stable *team API*: an API surrounding each team. An API (application programming interface) is a description and specification for how to interact programmatically with software, so we extend this idea to entire interactions with the team. The team API includes:

- Code: runtime endpoints, libraries, clients, UI, etc. produced by the team
- Versioning: how the team communicates changes to its code and services (e.g., using semantic versioning [SemVer] as a "team promise" not to break things)
- Wiki and documentation: especially how-to guides for the software owned by the team
- Practices and principles: the team's preferred ways of working
- Communication: the team's approach to remote communication tools, such as chat tools and video conferencing
- Work information: what the team is working on now, what's coming next, and overall priorities in the short to medium term
- Other: anything else that other teams need to use to interact with the team

The team API should explicitly consider usability by other teams: Will other teams find it easy and straightforward to interact with us, or will it be difficult and confusing? How easy will it be for a new team to get on board with our code and working practices? How do we respond to pull requests and other suggestions from other teams? Is our team backlog and product roadmap easily visible and understandable by other teams?

For effective team-first ownership of software, teams need to continuously define, advertise, test, and evolve their team API to ensure that it is fit for purpose for the consumers of that API: other teams. In *Dynamic Reteaming* (by Heidi Helfand), Evan Wiley, Director of Program Management at Pivotal Cloud Foundry (PCF), a major enterprise Platform-as-a-Service (PaaS) provider, describes how more than fifty teams are seen at PCF:

> We really try to maintain as much contract based, *API-based separation of concerns between teams* [emphasis added] as we can. We try not to share

code bases between teams. All the git repos for a particular team's feature are wholly owned by that team and if another team is going to make an addition or change to that code base, they'll either do it with a pull request or through cross-team pairing, where we would kind of send one half of a pair over to the dependency holding team and one half of that team's pair back to the upstream team to work on that feature.[28]

An even more stringent team API approach is taken at cloud vendor AWS, where CEO Jeff Bezos insisted on almost paranoid levels of separation between teams. For example, each team at AWS must assume that "every [other team] becomes a potential DOS [denial of service] attacker requiring service levels, quotas, and throttling."[29]

Many of the behaviors and patterns that make a good team API also make for a good platform and good team interactions in general. (See Chapter 5 for more details about what makes a good platform, and Chapter 7 for details about promise theory, a team-based approach to cooperation in sociotechnical systems.)

Facilitate Team Interactions for Trust, Awareness, and Learning

It is important to provide time, space, and money to enable and encourage people from different teams with similar skills and expertise to come together to learn from each other and to develop their professional competencies.

By explicitly setting aside time and space for teams and people to intercommunicate and learn, organizations can make learning and trust building part of the rhythm that facilitates effective team interactions. Two critical ways this can help teams build trust and awareness and learn new things are: (1) a consciously designed physical and virtual environment; and (2) time away from desks at guilds, communities of practice (a group of people who regularly get together on a voluntary basis to collectively learn and share knowledge about a domain of interest, internal tech conferences, etc.

Because this team interaction is outside the everyday building and running of the main software systems, Conway's law plays a much less obvious role, and a freer cross-association between teams can take place. Crucially, teams that have a chance to rehearse their team interactions in these contexts tend to find it easier to interact with other teams when building and running software systems, as found in the groundbreaking research by Robert Axelrod and author Mark Burgess.[30]

Explicitly Design the Physical and Virtual Environments to Help Team Interactions

Consciously designed physical and virtual environments are necessary for teams to learn and build trust. However, different people need different environments at different times to be productive. Some tasks (e.g., implementing and testing a complicated algorithm) might require full concentration and low levels of noise. Other tasks require a very collaborative approach (e.g., defining user stories and acceptance criteria). People who work all day with headphones on are seen as anti-social, and their behavior does not promote interaction and collaboration; but it could well be that the office environment is generally noisy and these people require a quiet environment to be effective.

Neither individual cubicles nor fully open-plan seating is generally suitable for teams: we need something better. Teams need the ability to collaborate frequently, internally and only occasionally externally (with other teams). This balance is hard to achieve both in an open-plan layout (no dedicated work area for the team) and in an individual-workspaces layout (time together needs to be planned ahead of time and meeting rooms are often scarce). Spotify recognized this early on in their growth and arranged their office space to support both needs.[31] Back in 2012, Henrik Kniberg and Anders Ivarsson—then working at Spotify—talked about how "squads in a tribe are all physically in the same office, normally right next to each other, and the lounge areas nearby promote collaboration between the squads."[32]

Office design for effective software delivery should accommodate all of the following modes of work: focused individual work, collaborative intra-team work, and collaborative inter-team work.

Having workspaces that clearly indicate the type of work going on also helps reduce disturbance and unnecessary interruptions.

CASE STUDY: TEAM-FOCUSED OFFICE SPACE AT CDL

Michael Lambert, Head of Development, CDL
Andy Rubio, Development Team Leader, CDL
CDL is a UK-based company that is a market leader in the highly competitive retail-insurance sector.

Here at CDL, our Agile journey has seen us evolve in many ways. One aspect many people are interested in is how we organize the working environment for our teams. From the start, we have always had the luxury of being able to colocate our Agile teams. After moving to new offices and then quickly outgrowing them, we moved many of our development project teams back to our old headquarters, which gave us multiple small project rooms where a development team could set up home. We liked the space and ownership this brought, but cross-team communication and visibility of other teams was less optimal. When our new home, "The Codeworks," was built, we thought long and hard about what the layout of the development areas should be.

We visualized everything, so lots of magnetic whiteboards [were] essential. We liked the team space our old building gave us, but we needed less isolation of teams, and we had the usual physical numbers and space constraints. If teams did not have enough space or only had small cubical clusters or tight horseshoe arrangements, then availability of meeting rooms for team ceremonies would become a big problem. Ideally, we wanted both: team space for the team to get their stuff done and openness for the teams to collaborate and share.

What we came up with was a "benched bay" approach, with one long bench for each team, and each bench was flanked by whiteboard partitions. Where a team butted up to an end wall, we painted it with smart-surface paint so we could draw on it (see Figure 3.4 on page 52).

The size and growth of teams is also an important factor in design. Some teams may be smaller while others may need to grow fast. The bench arrangement allowed for easy growth, especially if you haven't got supporting legs and pedestals in the way. Small teams could spread out while growing teams could squeeze up a bit. Of course, there is a limit on this. When the team is too big, we split it into two smaller teams, each taking functionally half of the backlog to make their own. The beauty of this is each team takes the culture of the old team with them, and they will diverge and grow themselves over time; but you can (with luck!) skip the "storming" and "norming" phases of starting a team from scratch. We deliberately have differing sizes of bays, where an extra table or two can be accommodated.

Initially, team benches were set centrally and symmetrically between the dividing whiteboard partitions, but we soon realized that an asymmetrical arrangement worked much better, where the bench was closer to one partition. This provided more space on one side to gather the team yet still allowed the opposite whiteboards to be used effectively.

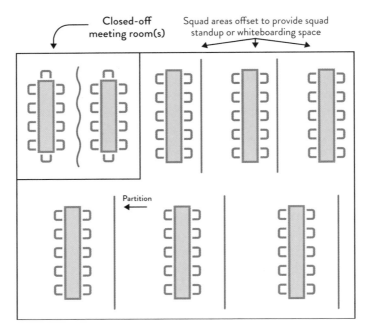

Figure 3.4: Office Layout at CDL

We used what we had learned from this arrangement when it came to fitting out the top floor for our new digital teams. Our original partitions were expensive, heavyweight structures that could only be moved at some expense. For the new digital space, we opted for lots of large, portable, but still substantial, whiteboards. Teams could now reposition and make breaks as they organized themselves.

This design is by no means perfect. All spaces are compromised in one way or another. We get things wrong, but we continue to learn and adapt. One such experiment was to remove the small glass partitions running down the center of the team benches. Another was to have height-adjustable sections on the ends of each set of benches for standing or for people who needed extra legroom.

As the case study from CDL shows, the physical work environment has a significant effect on the ability of teams to interact in useful ways. Successful organizations make sure to spend time and money achieving a good physical environment for their staff.

For example, the bank ING Netherlands explicitly redesigned its office space as part of a major organizational change around 2015 to align teams to value streams.[33] At ING, several stream-aligned "squads" working on similar products and services within a stream form a "tribe." Each tribe has a separate area within the office, including multiple team-sized spaces, one for each squad. The thought-out design of the office layout means that people from other squads or tribes can easily recognize aspects of other teams' work (such as kanban boards, WIP limits, status radiators, and so on) and rapidly learn new approaches. Some organizations have taken this even further, aligning entire floors of their office space to separate business streams, promoting high flow and easier collaboration within a stream.

Jeremy Brown from Red Hat Open Innovation Labs told us how they had everything on wheels (even plants!) in order to frequently reconfigure their physical environment for different types of work, and for teams to emerge and evolve their own space.[34] In their 2012 book *Make Space*, Scott Doorley and Scott Witthoft present many other creative ideas for arranging physical space in ways that ignite creativity and useful team interactions.[35]

CASE STUDY: STREAM-ALIGNED OFFICE LAYOUT FOR FLOW-BASED COLLABORATION AT AUTO TRADER

Dave Whyte, Operations Engineering Lead, Auto Trader
Andy Humphrey, Head of Customer Operations, Auto Trader

Back in 2013, as we started to move from a print-based business with many different offices around the country to a 100% digital business, we began to look at ways we could improve collaboration and optimize for the flow of work. We reorganized from fifteen offices into three, with our main office in Manchester, UK, on only two floors. The working environment was created to be as open plan as possible, with all senior managers sitting with their teams and no private offices. This made it much easier for people to communicate with each other, and we finally started bridging the gap between "the business" and IT.

Our new offices were built for collaboration, from the way the desks could be laid out to the limits on the number of monitor screens that one person could have at their desk (to avoid people "hiding" behind screens). Over the past few years, we have experimented with different office layouts and seating plans to help the right teams communicate and to promote flow:

- Organizing technical and non-technical teams on the same floors and in the same areas: This helped break down barriers between departments that shared the same goals and customers. The equipment given to sales, product, service, and technology became more aligned so that we could share tools more widely and work in the same way (e.g., all our sales and service colleagues have laptops; you don't have to be a rockstar developer to get a MacBook anymore).
- Clear-desk policy: We provided lockers for personal belongings and encouraged people to move around the office and sit where they needed to be that day in order to add value and not be limited to sitting at the same desk in the same team.
- Technology restrictions: The desks were designed with single monitors so that people could see those sitting opposite them and interact more freely. It was common for some technical staff to have two or three monitors, so this was not popular; but it's an interesting example of becoming a digital organization by actually restricting the use of some technology in order to meet the goal of being more collaborative. The desks even had recessed legs, creating a bench effect, so that people could move between them without snagging [their] legs—helping pairing and sitting with other people.
- Writable walls: To encourage more informal, creative conversations, the walls were made writable so that people could draw as they discussed, whether they were in a corridor or next to a car. Most meeting rooms were made of glass so that people could see who was in there and work out if they needed to be in there too. We also created more informal meeting spaces—sofas, soft chairs, etc.—so that people could sit down for a chat with a colleague without needing to plan a meeting room in advance.
- Event spaces: We also have event spaces designed into all our buildings, so we can get together as a company and even invite our local community by hosting events and meetups that help us get to know and work with people outside our organization.

We now have all the people in a certain business division sitting together. For example, private advertising is one of our business areas, handling vehicle sales by private individuals, and everyone involved in this stream of business sits on the same floor: marketing people, sales people, developers, testers, product managers, and so on. This means that everyone in the same business stream can "feel the pain" together and all decisions are more jointly owned. We have found that you start seeing things from other people's viewpoints when you sit with them.

Our office layout is quite deliberately designed to help flow and specific collaboration. We based our teams loosely on the model from Spotify, so we have squads of around eight people that build specific parts of a system, and collections of squads known as tribes. Each squad has its own team area located close to other squad areas from the same tribe. This enables squads from the same tribe to talk easily to each other—collaborating on similar parts of the system—while being physically separated from other tribes by walls and floors.

This layout helps teams focus on their business stream area, minimizing the need to talk with teams from other business areas to get their day-to-day work done. We bring teams together for cross-tribe learning by holding regular guild learning sessions and evening meetups.

The virtual environment is increasingly important as many organizations adopt a remote-first policy. The virtual environment comprises digital spaces such as a wiki, internal and external blogs and organization websites, chat tools, work tracking systems, and so forth. Effective remote work goes beyond having the necessary tools; teams need to agree on ground rules around working hours, response times, video conferencing, tone of communication, and other practical aspects that, if underestimated, can make or break a distributed team, even when all the right tools are available. In their 2013 book *Remote: Office Not Required*, Jason Fried and David Heinemeir Hansson go through how to address these and many other important aspects for remote teams.[36]

From an efficient-communication perspective, the virtual environment should be easy to navigate, guiding people to the right answer quickly. In particular, chat tools should have channel names or space names that are easy to predict and search for, with prefixes to group chats:

#deploy-pre-production

. . .

#practices-engineering
#practices-testing

. . .

#support-environments
#support-logging
#support-onboarding

. . .

#team-vesuvius
#team-kilimanjaro
#team-krakatoa

In a virtual environment, it can be useful to use naming conventions in usernames to make it easy for people to identify who's in a particular team, especially if that team is a central X-as-a-Service team, providing a platform or component (more on this in Chapter 5). Instead of simply "Jai Kale" as the display name within the chat tool and wiki, use something like "[Platform] Jai Kale" to identify that Jai Kale is in the platform team.

Warning: Engineering Practices Are Foundational

At the end of the day, technology teams need to invest in proven team practices like continuous delivery, test-first development, and a focus on software operability and releasability. Without them, all the effort invested in a team-first approach to work and flow will be greatly undermined or at least underachieved.

Continuous delivery practices support hypothesis-driven development and automation, operability practices provide early and ongoing operational checks and discovery, testability practices and test-first development enhance the design and fitness for purpose of solutions, and releasability practices ensure delivery pipelines are treated as a first-grade product. All of them are critical for fast flow and require an ongoing effort by all engineering teams.

Summary: Limit Teams' Cognitive Load and Facilitate Team Interactions to Go Faster

In a fast-changing and challenging context, teams are more effective than groups of individuals. Successful organizations—from the US military to corporations large and small—treat the team as the fundamental means of getting work done. Teams are generally small, stable, and long lived, allowing team members the time and space to develop their working patterns and team dynamics.

Importantly, due to limits on team size (Dunbar's number), there is an effective upper limit on the cognitive load that a single team can bear. This strongly suggests a limit on the size of the software systems and complexity of domains that any team should work with. The team needs to own the system or subsystems they are responsible for. Teams working on multiple codebases lack ownership and, especially, the mental space to understand and keep the corresponding systems healthy.

The team-first approach provides opportunities for many kinds of people to thrive in an organization. Instead of needing a thick skin or resilience in order to survive in an organization that atomizes individuals, people in a team-first organization have the space and support to develop their skills and practices within the context of a team.

Crucially, because communication between individuals is de-emphasized in favor of communication between teams for day-to-day work, the organization supports a wide range of communication preferences, from those people who communicate best one to one to those who like large group conversations. Furthermore, the effect of previously destructive individuals is curtailed. This humanistic approach is a huge benefit of choosing teams first.

PART II

Team Topologies that Work for Flow

KEY TAKEAWAYS

CHAPTER 4
- Ad hoc or constantly changing team design slows down software delivery.
- There is no single definitive team topology but several inadequate topologies for any one organization.
- Technical and cultural maturity, org scale, and engineering discipline are critical aspects when considering which topology to adopt.
- In particular, the feature-team/product-team pattern is powerful but only works with a supportive surrounding environment.
- Splitting a team's responsibilities can break down silos and empower other teams.

CHAPTER 5
- The four fundamental team topologies simplify modern software team interactions.
- Mapping common industry team types to the fundamental topologies sets up organizations for success, removing gray areas of ownership and overloaded/underloaded teams.
- The main topology is (business) stream-aligned; all other topologies support this type.
- The other topologies are enabling, complicated-subsystems, and platform.
- The topologies are often "fractal" (self-similar) at large scale: teams of teams.

CHAPTER 6
- Choose software boundaries using a team-first approach.
- Beware of hidden monoliths and coupling in the software-delivery chain.
- Use software boundaries defined by business-domain bounded contexts.
- Consider alternative software boundaries when necessary and suitable.

Static Team Topologies

Instead of structuring teams according to technical know-how or activities, organize teams according to business domain areas.
—**Jutta Eckstein,** "Feature Teams—Distributed and Dispersed,"
in *Agility Across Time and Space*

In Part I, we saw the strong pull that Conway's law exercises on system architecture by mirroring team structures and communication paths in the final product design. We also highlighted that efficient software delivery requires a team-first approach that relies on long-lived autonomous teams achieving fast flow. Part II will focus on how we put these two ideas together in a way that maximizes flow yet respects the cognitive limits of teams.

In Chapter 4, we start with the need to intentionally design teams, and to understand that good and bad team patterns are a factor of many aspects, like org size, maturity, and software scale. Today, the prevailing way to set up or reorganize teams is ad hoc, focused on immediate needs rather than the ability to adapt in the long run.

In order to be as effective as possible, we need to *consciously* design our teams rather than merely allow them to form accidentally or haphazardly. We call these consciously designed team structures team topologies, a term that acknowledges that teams should be deliberately "placed" into organizations while also referring to the boundary of responsibility of each team.

In this chapter, we'll take a look at examples of static team topologies—that is team structures and interactions that fit a specific organization's context at a given point in time. In particular, we will draw from the catalog of

DevOps Topologies, which makes for a good, approachable starting point for many organizations.

But first, let's look at a couple of common anti-patterns that result from ad hoc team design.

Team Anti-Patterns

As we've seen so far, the way in which people are organized into teams for building and operating software systems has a strong effect on the nature of the resulting systems, following Conway's law.

When organizations do not explicitly think about team structures and patterns of interaction, they encounter unexpected difficulties building and running software systems. In our work with clients, we've seen the occurrence of two particular anti-patterns for team formation across organizations of different sizes.

The first anti-pattern is ad hoc team design. This includes teams that have grown too large and been broken up as the communication overhead starts taking a toll, teams created to take care of all COTS software or all middleware, or a DBA team created after a software crash in production due to poor database handling. Of course, all of these situations should trigger some action, but without considering the broader context of the interrelationships between teams, what seems like a natural solution might slow down delivery and eat away at the autonomy of teams.

The other common anti-pattern is shuffling team members. This leads to extremely volatile team assembled on a project basis and disassembled immediately afterward, perhaps leaving one or two engineers behind to handle the "hardening" and maintenance phases of the application(s). While there is a sense of higher flexibility and a perceived ability to respond faster to deadlines, the cost of forming new teams and switching context repeatedly gets overlooked (or is unconsciously factored in the project estimates). A computer will perform the same whether it is placed in Room A or Room B, but an engineer placed on Team A may perform very differently than if placed on Team B.

Organizations must design teams intentionally by asking these questions: Given our skills, constraints, cultural and engineering maturity, desired software architecture, and business goals, which team topology will help us deliver results faster and safer? How can we reduce or avoid handovers between teams in the main flow of change? Where should the boundaries be in the software system in order to preserve system viability and encourage rapid flow? How can our teams align to that?

Design for Flow of Change

Organizations that build and run large-scale software systems are turning to organization designs that emphasize the flow of change from concept to working software—what we might call "low friction" software delivery. Older organizational models—with functional silos between different departments, heavy use of outsourcing, and repeated hand-offs between teams—do not provide the safety at speed or the organizational feedback mechanisms necessary for the ongoing evolution of business services needed to respond to customer and market conditions on a daily basis. As Naomi Stanford points out, "an organization has a better chance of success if it is reflectively designed."[1]

Spotify provides a good example of explicit organizational design to improve the effectiveness of software delivery and operations, as described by Henrik Kniberg and Anders Ivarsson in their 2012 blog post, "Scaling Agile @ Spotify."[2] Known as "The Spotify Model," technical staff at Spotify are arranged into small, autonomous, cross-functional squads, each with a long-term mission and comprised of around five to nine people. Several squads that work on similar areas are collected into a tribe, a sort of affinity grouping of squads. The squads within a tribe are familiar with the work of other squads and coordinate inside the tribe.

Engineers within a tribe with similar skills and competencies share practices through a chapter. So, for example, all the testers across six squads in a tribe could be part of a testers chapter. Line management also happens via chapters, but the line manager (the chapter lead) is also part of the day-to-day work of a squad, not an aloof manager. Spotify also uses a more diffuse "guild," akin to a community of practice, that can include people from across multiple tribes, chapters, and squads. "Chapters and guilds…[are] the glue that keeps the company together, [providing] economies of scale without sacrificing too much autonomy."[3]

Many organizations have mistakenly copied the Spotify model without understanding the underlying purpose, culture, dynamics, or trajectory of the Spotify team arrangements. As Kniberg and Ivarsson clearly state in their post: "We didn't invent this model. Spotify is (like any good Agile company) evolving fast. This article is only a snapshot of our current way of working—a journey in progress, not a journey completed."[4]

It is essential that organizations take into account more than a static placement of people when looking at the design of team interactions.

Shape Team Intercommunication to Enable Flow and Sensing

Many organizations have significant flaws in the way their teams interact as part of building and running software systems. Specifically, such organizations seem to assume that software delivery is a one-way process, leading from specification to design, from design to coding, from coding to testing and releasing, and from releasing to business as usual (BAU) operation (see Figure 4.1).

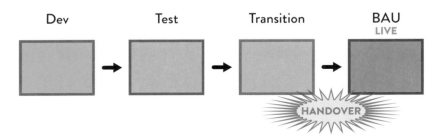

Figure 4.1: Organization not Optimized for Flow of Change
Traditional flow of change in an organization not optimized for flow, with a
series of groups owning different activities and handing over the work to the next team.
No information flows back from the live systems into teams building the software.

This linear, stepwise sequence of changes—usually with separate functional silo divisions for each stage—(as seen in Figure 4.1)—is completely incompatible with the speed of change and complexity of modern software systems. The assumption that the software-development process has little or nothing to learn from how the software runs in the live environment is fundamentally flawed. On the contrary, organizations that expose software-development teams to the software running in the live environment tend to address user-visible and operational problems much more rapidly compared to their siloed competitors (see Figure 4.2 on page 65).

In *Accelerate*, Nicole Forsgren, Jez Humble, and Gene Kim collected data on the software-development practices of hundreds of organizations around the world, which led them to conclude that "we must...ensure delivery teams are cross-functional, with all the skills necessary to design, develop, test, deploy, and operate the system on the same team."[5] Organizations that value information feedback from live (production) systems can not only improve their software more rapidly but also develop a heightened responsiveness to customers and users.

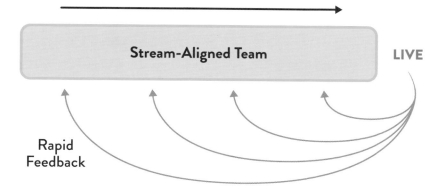

Figure 4.2: Organization Optimized for Flow of Change
Organizations set up for fast flow avoid hand-offs by keeping work within the
stream-aligned team, and they ensure that the rich set of operational information
flows back into the team.

This superior "sensing" ability comes from treating frontline staff and
teams as highly valuable sources of signals about the market and environment
in which the organization is operating.

When we apply this kind of sensing not only at the edges of the organization but also *inside* the organization—between teams—we can provide a
radically enhanced strategic capability for rapidly discovering deficiencies in
platforms, services, and interfaces, enabling us to address these problems early
and thereby improve the effectiveness of IT as a whole. (We will look further at
this organizational sensing in Part III.)

DevOps and the DevOps Topologies

This kind of organizational sensing "nirvana," with cross-functional teams that
build, test, and operate their own software, was an unfamiliar concept to most
organizations back in 2009. By then, the classic anti-pattern in team design
and interactions of completely separating responsibilities between development and operations teams (among others) was prevalent, with software
releases being thrown over the "fence" or "wall" and communication mostly
accomplished through tickets. In the DevOps world, this became known as the
"wall of confusion."

The DevOps movement emerged around 2009 due to this growing friction between Dev and Ops, highlighted by an increased pressure on operations

teams to deploy more often as Agile became more mainstream. The problem was that many organizations adopting Agile were not explicitly addressing the gap between software delivery speed and operations teams' capacity to provide resources or deploy updates. The misalignment between teams became more and more evident, leading to poor behaviors and lack of focus on the flow of work.

A key contribution of DevOps was to raise awareness of the problems lingering in how teams interacted (or not) across the delivery chain, causing delays, rework, failures, and a lack of understanding and empathy toward other teams. It also became clear that such issues were not only happening between application development and operations teams but in interactions with many other teams involved in software delivery, like QA, InfoSec, networking, and more.

Even though many people see DevOps as fundamentally addressing technological aspects of automation and tooling, only organizations that also address fundamental misalignments between teams are able to achieve the full potential benefits from adopting DevOps.

DevOps Topologies

The DevOps Topologies catalog, originally created by Matthew Skelton in 2013 and later expanded by Manuel Pais, is an online collection of team design and interactions patterns and anti-patterns that work well for kick-starting conversations around team responsibilities, interfaces, and collaboration between technology teams.[6] Crucially, successful patterns are strongly dependent on contextual aspects, like organization and product size, engineering maturity, and shared goals.

The topologies became an effective reference of team structures for enterprise software delivery; however, they were never meant to be static structures, but rather a depiction of a moment in time influenced by multiple factors, like the type of products delivered, technical leadership, and operational experience. The implicit idea was that teams should evolve and morph over time.

This chapter presents some of the patterns in the DevOps Topologies catalog to help illustrate the thinking around choosing team structures with organization context and needs in mind. It is not intended to be a deep dive into the DevOps Topologies that are available online; instead, it is a helpful introduction to team design for technology teams applied to DevOps. The rest of the book will focus on the broader context of business and technology teams at large, beyond DevOps.

The DevOps Topologies reflect two key ideas: (1) There is no one-size-fits-all approach to structuring teams for DevOps success. The suitability and effectiveness of any given topology depends on the organization's context. (2) There are several topologies known to be detrimental (anti-patterns) to DevOps success, as they overlook or go against core tenets of DevOps. In short, there is no "right" topology, but several "bad" topologies for any one organization.

Successful Team Patterns

An inadequate choice of topology doesn't necessarily mean that the desired outcomes aren't good. It's often the case that a given topology doesn't yield those outcomes because there is a focus on the new team structure but not enough consideration about the *surrounding* teams and structures. The success of different types of teams does not depend solely on team members's skills and experience; it also depends on (perhaps most importantly) the surrounding environment, teams, and interactions.

Feature Teams Require High-Engineering Maturity and Trust

Let's take the example of feature teams. We consider a feature team to be a cross-functional, cross-component team that can take a customer facing feature from idea all the way to production, making them available to customers and, ideally, monitoring its usage and performance. Are these a pattern or an anti-pattern? As you might have guessed by now, it depends.

A cross-functional feature team can bring high value to an organization by delivering cross-component, customer-centric features much faster than multiple component teams making their own changes and synchronizing into a single release. But this can only happen when the feature team is self-sufficient, meaning they are able to deliver features into production without waiting for other teams.

The feature team typically needs to touch multiple codebases, which might be owned by different component teams. If the team does not have a high degree of engineering maturity, they might take shortcuts, such as not automating tests for new user workflows or not following the "boy-scout rule" (leaving the code better than they found it). Over time, this leads to a breakdown of trust between teams as technical debt increases and slows down delivery speed.

A lack of ownership over shared code may result from the cumulative effects of several teams working on the same codebase unless inter-team discipline is high.

Around 2015, Ericsson moved to a DevOps approach to building and running software for emerging telecom business areas, such as "Software-Defined Networking" or "Network Functions Virtualization."[7] Teams in this space became responsible for developing and supporting their software in production.

Some of Ericsson's large-scale projects, comprised of multiple subsystems, require teams working across multiple sites. Each team is composed of five to nine members, and a single subsystem might be developed by multiple teams. However, teams must include all the core capabilities/roles to develop and maintain their own features in a largely independent fashion. Occasionally, very large features are worked on simultaneously by a few colocated teams, acting as a single, larger feature team.

However, while inter-team communication and dependencies were greatly reduced with teams working on intra-subsystem features, someone still had to keep oversight of the system as a whole and ensure subsystems integrated and interacted according to the desired user experience, performance, and reliability. Therefore, specific roles were created, such as system architects, system owners, or integration leads. Crucially, people in these roles work across the entire project/organization sort of like "communication conduits," with direct and frequent interaction with feature teams. They support them on cross-subsystem concerns (such as interfaces and integration) to allow them to maintain a regular feature delivery cadence.

Product Teams Need a Support System

Product teams (identical in purpose and characteristics to a feature team but owning the entire set of features for one or more products) still depend on infrastructure, platform, test environments, build systems, and delivery pipelines (and more) for their work to become available to end users. They might have full control over some of these dependencies, but they will likely need help with others due to the natural cognitive and expertise limits of a team (as explained in Chapter 3).

The key for the team to remain autonomous is for external dependencies to be non-blocking, meaning that new features don't sit idle, waiting for something to happen beyond the control of the team. For example, it's extremely difficult to ensure that a separate QA team will be available to evaluate a new feature exactly when the product team finishes it. Teams have different work-loads, priorities, and problems; and generally, there's too much uncertainty in building and running software systems for a pre-defined schedule to succeed in coordinating multiple teams on the same stream of work. Insisting on this approach inevitably leads to wait times and delays.

Non-blocking dependencies often take the form of self-service capabilities (e.g., around provisioning test environments, creating deployment pipelines, monitoring, etc.) developed and maintained by other teams. These can be consumed independently by the product teams when they need them.

For example, Microsoft has been using product teams since the 1980s. With the availability of Azure as an IaaS and PaaS solution for Microsoft products and services, teams within Microsoft are able to consume infrastructure and platform features "as a service." This allows teams to significantly increase delivery speed. In particular, the teams building the Visual Studio product have undergone a radical transformation from a desktop-first, multi-month delivery cycle, to a cloud-first, daily/weekly delivery cycle.[8]

Creating product teams without a compatible support system, consisting of easy-to-consume services (preferably via a platform-oriented approach) and readily available expertise for tasks that the team is unfamiliar with, creates more bottlenecks. Product teams end up frequently waiting on "hard dependencies" to functional teams (such as infrastructure, networking, QA). There is increased friction as product teams are pressured to deliver faster, but they are part of a system that does not support the necessary levels of autonomy.

Cloud Teams Don't Create Application Infrastructure

Cloud teams that are, for the most part, a rebranding of traditional infrastructure teams will fail to take advantage of the speed and scalability that the cloud offers. If the cloud team simply mimics the current behaviors and infrastructure processes, the organization will incur the same delays and bottlenecks for software delivery as before.

Product teams need autonomy to provision their own environments and resources in the cloud, creating new images and templates where necessary. The cloud team might still own the provisioning process—ensuring that the necessary controls, policies, and auditing are in place (especially in highly regulated industries)—but their focus should be in providing high-quality self-services that match both the needs of product teams and the need for adequate risk and compliance management.

In other words, there needs to be a split between the responsibility of designing the cloud infrastructure process (by the cloud team) and the actual provisioning and updates to application resources (by the product teams).

SRE Makes Sense at Scale

Site Reliability Engineering is an approach to the operation and improvement of software applications pioneered by Google to deal with their global, multi-million-user systems. If adopted in full, SRE is significantly different from IT operations of the past, due to its focus on the "error budget" (namely defining what is an acceptable amount of downtime) and the ability of SRE teams to push back on poor software.

People on SRE teams need excellent coding skills and—crucially—a strong drive (and bandwidth) to automate repetitive Ops tasks using code, thereby continually reducing toil. Ben Treynor, Vice President of Engineering at Google, said that SRE is "what happens when you ask a software engineer to design an operations function."[9]

The SRE model sets up a healthy and productive interaction between the development and SRE teams by using service-level objectives (SLOs) and error budgets to balance the speed of new features with whatever work is needed to make the software reliable.

> **TIP**
>
> **SRE teams are not essential; they are optional.**
> That's right: not every development team at Google uses SRE. "Downscale the SRE support if your project is shrinking in scale, and finally let your development team own the SRE work if the scale doesn't require SRE support," said Jaana B. Dogan, SRE at Google.[10]

The SRE approach is a highly dynamic approach to building and running large-scale software systems. The SRE team has several different interactions with application development teams at different times, depending on various factors: how many users the software application has, how reliable the software is, how available the software needs to be from a product perspective, etc. Figure 4.3 illustrates this.

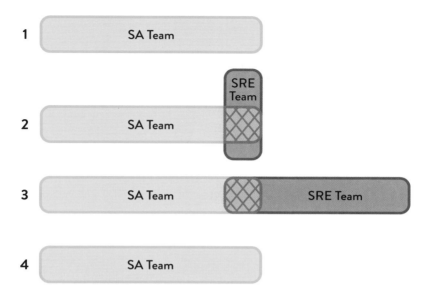

Figure 4.3: Relationship between SRE Team and Application Team

The relationship between an SRE team and an application-development team changes at different points of the software's life and even month by month. Initially (#1 in Figure 4.3), the application development team alone builds and runs the software in production until the scale merits SRE help. During a second stage (#2 in Figure 4.3), as the application usage increases, SRE provides guidance (represented in green) to the application development team on how to make the application work better at global scale. Later, SRE becomes fully involved by running and supporting the application (but still collaborating with the application team) when the scale merits it (#3 in Figure 4.3). At this point, the product owner for the application must decide a suitable service-level objective with a corresponding error budget. If at some point (#4 in Figure 4.3) the application becomes too difficult to support due to lack of operability, or if the application usage drops off, the application team takes on operational responsibility again. If the application's

SRE teams have a strong relationship with one or more application-development team, a kind of affinity. In this respect, we can see the SRE model as a special kind of stream-aligned team.

operability improves sufficiently (to meet the error budget) and application usage also increases, the relationship might go back to stage #3.

The dynamic interaction between SRE and application-development teams is part of what makes the SRE approach work so well for Google and similar organizations: it recognizes that building and running software systems is a sociotechnical activity, not an assembly line in a factory.

The SRE model is not an easy option, however. Dave Rensin, Director of Customer Reliability Engineering at Google Cloud, says "achieving Google-class operational rigor requires a sustained commitment on your part."[11] SRE is a dynamic balance between a commitment to operability from the application-development team and expertise from the SRE team. Without a high degree of engineering discipline and commitment from management, this fine balance in SRE can easily degrade into a traditional "us and them" silo that leads to repeated service outages and mistrust between teams.

Considerations When Choosing a Topology

An organization's context influences the successful setup of certain types of teams, as is apparent from the many team-structure examples we just provided. Next, we will outline different factors to take into account when selecting a topology.

Technical and Cultural Maturity

Organizations at different stages of technical and cultural maturity will find different team structures to be effective. For example, by 2013, both Amazon and Netflix had a well-established strategy, using cross-functional teams with end-to-end responsibility for the services they provided to the rest of the organization.[12]

Meanwhile, traditional organizations adopting Agile—moving to smaller batches of delivery—often lacked the mature engineering practices required to keep a sustainable pace over time (such as automated testing, deployment, or monitoring). They could benefit from a temporary DevOps team with battle-tested engineers to bring in expertise and, more importantly, bring teams together by collaborating on shared practices and tools.

However, without a clear mission and expiration date for such a DevOps team, it's easy to cross the thin line between this pattern and the corresponding anti-pattern of yet another silo (DevOps team) with compartmentalized knowledge (such as configuration management, monitoring, deployment strategies, and others) in the organization.

On the other hand, for a large enterprise where successful DevOps adoption across the board requires both top-down and bottom-up alignment, it makes sense to invest in a team of DevOps evangelists that raise awareness and are vocal about initial achievements in other parts of the organization.

Organization Size, Software Scale, and Engineering Maturity

As we've seen, choosing a good team topology is highly dependent on the situational context of the organization and teams within it. At the very least, organization size (or software scale) and engineering maturity should influence which topologies are chosen in a DevOps context, as shown in Figure 4.4.

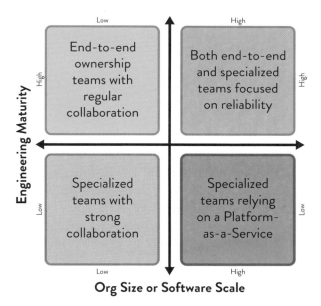

Figure 4.4: Influence of Size and Engineering Maturity on Choice of Topologies
Organization size (or software scale) and engineering discipline influence the effectiveness of team interaction patterns.

Low maturity organizations will need time to acquire the engineering and product development capabilities required for autonomous end-to-end teams. Meanwhile, more specialized teams (development, operations, security, and others) are an acceptable trade-off, as long as they collaborate closely to minimize wait times and quickly address issues. For a moderate scale of organization or software, patterns that emphasize close collaboration between teams at speed work well. As the size of the organization or software scale increases, focusing on providing the underlying infrastructure or platform as a service brings important benefits in terms of user-facing service reliability and the ability to meet customer expectations. If the organization has a high level of engineering maturity and discipline, then the SRE model described earlier may be effective at scale as well.

Splitting Responsibilities to Break Down Silos

Sometimes we can remove or lessen dependencies on specific teams by breaking down their set of responsibilities and empowering other teams to take some of them on. For example, a pattern increasingly adopted in many organizations over the past few years has been to separate the activities of database development (DB Dev) from database administration (DBA).

The activities of DB Dev and DBA had often been joined in a functional silo of the database team, but the need for more rapid flow of change, coupled with a reduction in the use of shared databases, makes it more effective to split these roles. In practice, the DBA role typically becomes part of a platform, whether internally run or as part of a cloud provider's Database-as-a-Service offering. (See Chapter 5 for more details about platforms.)

All the examples we mentioned so far highlight the importance of thinking about teams' capabilities (or lack thereof) and how that causes dependencies between teams. Instead of simply replicating teams or adding more people when workload increases, it's important to think about which dependencies between teams we should remove and which we should explicitly accept, because we see more benefits than disadvantages. (See Chapter 5 and Chapter 7 for more details about the relationships between teams.)

Dependencies and Wait Times between Teams

To achieve teams that have well-defined responsibilities, can work independently, and are optimized for flow, it is essential to detect and track dependencies and wait times between teams. In *Making Work Visible*, Dominica DeGrandis recommends the use of a Physical Dependency Matrix or "dependency tags" on kanban cards to identify and track dependencies, and infer the communication needed to make these dependencies work well: "Visualizing important cross-team information helps communicate across teams."[13]

In their 2012 paper, "A Taxonomy of Dependencies in Agile Software Development," Diane Strode and Sid Huff propose three different categories of dependency: knowledge, task, and resource dependencies.[14] Such a taxonomy can help pinpoint dependencies between teams and the potential constraints to the flow of work ahead of time.

Whichever tool is used, it is important to track the number of dependencies per area, and to establish thresholds and alerts that are meaningful for a particular situation. The number of dependencies should not be allowed to increase unchecked. Instead, such an increase should trigger adjustments in the team design and dependencies.

> **TIP**
>
> **Detect and track interdependencies.**
> Spotify relies on a simple spreadsheet to detect and track interdependencies between squads and tribes. It highlights whether a dependency is on a squad within the same tribe (acceptable) or in a different tribe (potentially a warning that team design or work assignment is wrong). The tool also tracks how soon the dependency will impact the flow of the depending team.

Using DevOps Topologies to Evolve the Organization

So far we've addressed multiple aspects that impact the effectiveness of certain topologies at a given point in time. But organizations, teams, and strategies change over time, either via an intentional course of action (e.g., DevOps dojos to improve teams' cultural and engineering maturity) or due to changes in markets and technology.

While many organizations looked at the DevOps Topologies catalog for "snapshot" advice on effective team structures, some went a couple of steps further by thinking of an evolutionary path, from a topology that makes the most sense in today's context to an end goal that matches expected changes in organizational capabilities and constraints.

What follows are a couple of industry examples of DevOps transformations strongly influenced by evolving DevOps Topologies over time to adapt to new contexts.

Pulak Agrawal, Continuous Delivery Architext, and Jonathan Hammant, UKI DevOps Lead, told us firsthand how they've used the DevOps Topologies patterns to evolve organizations Accenture consults for—in particular, at a healthcare client they started with a DevOps team back in April 2017. They soon realized they had fallen into an anti-pattern because the tooling expertise brought in by the DevOps team ended up in a silo.

In January 2018, they evolved their team structures in order to bring development, operations, and the DevOps tooling team closer together. Pulak described to us how this took place:

> We delivered an Infrastructure as Code (IaC) project on our client's Azure infrastructure, automatically installing, configuring, and operating an enterprise document management product. We utilized an "Ops as Infrastructure-as-a-Service" pattern for this project. This included early involvement from the Ops team who were checking in operational code and developers who focused on non-functional production requirements from day one. Individuals from the siloed tooling team from the earlier stage were present to help support the infrastructure while this happened.[15]

A third stage of evolution aimed to build on their earlier success and fully transition the DevOps team from an execution role to an evangelizing one, so that development and operations teams would become self-sufficient and collaborate around automation of the required steps. Pulak explained:

> The [DevOps] team is now evolving into a "DevOps Evangelists team" pattern, working with the client to educate and enable the individual project teams, so they make themselves obsolete along the way. They will automate the development and operations steps, implement monitoring and alerting solutions. They will then look to make development and operations own the automation and execution of it themselves.[16]

In Part III of the book, we will look in more detail at the evolution of team topologies in a broader context, beyond DevOps.

CASE STUDY: EVOLUTION OF TEAM TOPOLOGIES AT TRANSUNION (PART 1)

Ian Watson, Head of DevOps, TransUnion

TransUnion (formerly Callcredit) is the UK's second largest credit reference agency (CRA), with international offices in Spain, the US, Dubai, and

Lithuania. They provide expert services for managing consumer data for businesses across every sector around the world, helping businesses and consumers make more informed, confident decisions.

Ian Watson, Head of DevOps at TransUnion from 2015 to 2018, recalls how the DevOps Topologies helped them guide their growth over time.

In 2014, our technology group within TransUnion began a major expansion to meet growing demand for software-based analytical solutions. We knew that in order to scale effectively, we had to consider the interrelationships between different technology teams. We turned to the DevOps Topologies patterns to help us plan out our digital transformation. We wanted to bring development (Dev) and operations (Ops) closer together but avoid a separate "DevOps team." Instead, we adopted a hybrid model, with two temporary DevOps teams collaborating to help bring Dev and Ops together over time.

We realized that our DevOps journey at TransUnion needed to be based on the evolution of team relationships, not a static reconfiguration. The DevOps Topologies patterns helped us to reason about how our digital transformation would happen and accelerated our adoption of cloud technologies and automation approaches. The patterns helped us avoid some pitfalls, like a separate DevOps team, and helped define team responsibilities more effectively. We've been able to scale our technology division significantly over the past four years, with great results.

Summary: Adopt and Evolve Team Topologies that Match Your Current Context

Setting up new team structures and responsibilities reactively, triggered by the need to scale a product, adopt new technologies, or respond to new market demands, can help in the present moment but often fails to achieve the speed and efficiency of well thought-out topologies.

Because those decisions are often made on an individual team basis, they lack consideration for important organization-wide factors, like technical and cultural maturity, organization size, scale of the software, engineering disciple, or inter-team dependencies. The result is team structures optimized for problems that are temporary or limited in scope, rather than adaptive to new problems over time.

The "DevOps team" anti-pattern is a quintessential example. On paper, it makes sense to bring automation and tooling experts in house to accelerate the delivery and operations of our software. However, this team can quickly become a hard dependency for application teams if the DevOps team is being asked to execute steps on the delivery path of every application, rather than helping to design and build self-service capabilities that application teams can rely on autonomously.

It is critical to explicitly consider the different aspects at play and adopt topologies that work given the organizational context (which tends to evolve slowly), rather than adapting those that solve a particular problem or need in a given moment in time.

In particular, within a DevOps context the DevOps Topologies can help shed some light on which topologies work well for which contexts. Forward-thinking organizations take a multi-stage approach to their team design, understanding that what works best today might not necessarily be the case in a few years, or even months from now.

5

The Four Fundamental Team Topologies

The architecture of the system gets cemented in the forms of the teams that develop it.

—**Ruth Malan**, "Conway's Law"

In many organizations, there is a variety of team types and there are even teams taking on multiple roles (e.g., an infrastructure and tooling team). This sprawl makes it hard for everyone to visualize the full organizational landscape: Do we have the right teams in place? Are we lacking capabilities in some areas that are not being addressed by any team? Does it look like teams have the necessary balance between autonomy and support by other teams?

Answering these questions becomes simpler if we reduce the number of team variations to four fundamental team topologies:

- Stream-aligned team
- Enabling team
- Complicated-subsystem team
- Platform team

When used with care, these are the only four team topologies needed to build and run modern software systems. When combined with effective software boundaries (as presented in Chapter 6) and team interactions (as presented in Chapter 7), the restriction of these four team types acts as a powerful template for effective organization design (see Figure 5.1 on page 80).

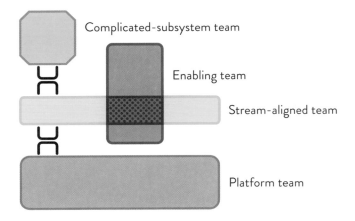

Complicated-subsystem team

Enabling team

Stream-aligned team

Platform team

Figure 5.1: The Four Fundamental Team Topologies

The four fundamental team topologies—stream aligned, enabling, complicated subsystem, and platform—should act as "magnets" for all team types. All teams should move toward one of these four magnetic poles; that is, we should prefer these types, and aim to adopt the purpose, role, responsibility, and interaction behavior of these fundamental types for every team in our organization. Simplifying the types of teams to just these four helps to reduce ambiguity within the organization. As was identified by Jiao Luo and colleagues in research published in 2018, reduced ambiguity around organizational roles is a key part of success in modern organization design.[1]

A large or mid-sized organization is likely to have one or more teams of each fundamental topology; multiple stream-aligned teams are the starting point (as we will see in this chapter), but an organization may also have several platform teams, a few enabling teams for different purposes (perhaps one addressing CI/CD and a second addressing infrastructure or architecture), and, if strictly necessary, one or two complicated-subsystem teams.

NOTE

Where is the Ops team? Where is the support team?

There is no "Ops" team or "support" team in the fundamental topologies, and this is deliberate. The long-lived teams building the systems are very close to the live operation of the systems they are building. There is no "handover" to a separate Ops or support team; even with the SRE pattern (see Chapter 4), the teams are closely aligned. Stream-aligned teams follow good software-delivery practices (like continuous delivery and operability), and they are responsible for live operation, even if very little code is being written. In effect, Ops and support are largely aligned to streams. (We will go into how successful organizations manage support activities in the context of rapid, safe flow of change later in this chapter.)

Now let's go into more detail on each of the four fundamental team topologies.

Stream-Aligned Teams

A "stream" is the continuous flow of work aligned to a business domain or organizational capability. Continuous flow requires clarity of purpose and responsibility so that multiple teams can coexist, each with their own flow of work.

A stream-aligned team is a team aligned to a single, valuable stream of work; this might be a single product or service, a single set of features, a single user journey, or a single user persona. Further, the team is empowered to build and deliver customer or user value as quickly, safely, and independently as possible, without requiring hand-offs to other teams to perform parts of the work.

The stream-aligned team is the primary team type in an organization, and the purpose of the other fundamental team topologies is to reduce the burden on the stream-aligned teams. As we see later in this chapter, the mission of an enabling team, for instance, is to help stream-aligned teams acquire missing capabilities, taking on the effort of research and trials, and setting up successful practices. The mission of a platform team is to reduce the cognitive load of stream-aligned teams by off-loading lower level detailed knowledge (e.g., provisioning, monitoring, or deployment), providing easy-to-consume services around them.

Because a stream-aligned team works on the full spectrum of delivery, they are, by necessity, closer to the customer and able to quickly incorporate feedback from customers while monitoring their software in production. Such a team can react to system problems in near real-time, steering the work as needed. In the words of Don Reinertsen: "In product development, we can change direction more quickly when we have a small team of highly skilled people instead of a large team."[2]

Different streams can coexist in an organization: specific customer streams, business-area streams, geography streams, product streams, user-persona streams, or even compliance streams (in highly regulated industries). (See Chapter 6 for details on how to organize work along these different types of streams.) A stream can even take the form of a micro-enterprise within a large firm, with an independent focus and purpose (e.g., innovating on products that do not exist yet). Whichever kind of stream of changes a stream-aligned team is aligned to, that team is funded in a long-term, sustainable manner as part of a portfolio or program of work, not as a fleeting project.

In a modern software organization, we expect most teams to be stream aligned. The flow of work is clear, and each stream has a steady, expectable flow of work for the stream-aligned team to prioritize.

This stands in stark contrast to traditional work allocation, whereby either a large request by a single customer or a set of smaller requests by multiple customers get translated into a project. Once the project is approved and funded, several teams will potentially get involved (e.g., front-end, back-end, and DBA teams) and be required to fit the new work into their existing backlog.

CASE STUDY: STRICTLY INDEPENDENT SERVICE TEAMS AT AMAZON

As far back as 2002, Amazon adopted a team topology that used highly independent teams. This was a deliberate mandate from CEO Jeff Bezos to ensure that each service or application in the Amazon estate was truly independent—acknowledging Conway's law—and ensured that the teams would be independent as well.[3] Amazon is also known for limiting the size of its software teams to those that can be fed by two pizzas, in order to increase accountability and maximize speed of delivery and discovery.[4]

Around 2002, Jeff Bezos' sent a mandate to the Amazon engineering division that set out very specific rules for team organization:[5]

- Each team is fully responsible for developing and operating its own service (whereby a service can be seen as one or more features of Amazon.com or AWS products).

- Each service is provided through an API, either for internal or external consumption; teams do not interfere or make any assumptions on other teams' services architecture or technology.

In line with the principle "you build it, you run it" popularized by Werner Vogels, CTO of Amazon, "service teams" (as they're called internally) must be cross-functional and include all the required capabilities to manage, specify, design, develop, test, and operate their services (including infrastructure provisioning and client support). These capabilities are not necessarily mapped to individuals; the team as a whole must provide them. Each individual has a primary area of expertise, but their contributions are not limited to it.

There is very little coordination required between service teams, leading to a highly distributed and heterogeneous stack of microservices. Interestingly, there is an exception for testing, as software development engineers in testing (SDETs) work across the whole organization, looking to promote good testing practices and tools across teams (but each team has the day-to-day testing role embedded). They also ensure a smooth cross-service, cross-device, cross-geography user experience. The SDET role provides the kind of valuable input provided by people in a productivity or tooling team, facilitating and encouraging good practices across teams.

The Amazon two-pizza-team model is an example of stream-aligned teams: the teams are substantially independent, have ownership over their services, and have responsibility for the runtime success of the software they write. The fact that Amazon has been using this model for over seventeen years shows how effective it can be to align teams to independent streams of change.

Capabilities within a Stream-Aligned Team

Generally speaking, each stream-aligned team will require a set of capabilities in order to progress work from its initial (requirements) exploration stages to production. These capabilities include (but are not restricted to):

- Application security
- Commercial and operational viability analysis

- Design and architecture
- Development and coding
- Infrastructure and operability
- Metrics and monitoring
- Product management and ownership
- Testing and quality assurance
- User experience (UX)

It's critical not to assume each capability maps to an individual role in the team; that would mean teams would have to include at least nine members to match the list above. Instead, we're talking about being able, as a team, to understand and act upon the above capabilities. This might mean having a mix of generalists and a few specialists. Having only specialized roles would lead to a bottleneck every time a piece of work depended on a specialist who might be currently busy.

> **NOTE**
>
> Site Reliability Engineering (SRE) teams, pioneered by Google, are really a special kind of stream-aligned team in the sense that they are responsible for the reliability of large-scale applications running in production. SRE teams interact primarily with one or more stream-aligned teams responsible for developing applications, and the flow of software change is very much aligned to a stream.

Why Stream-Aligned Team, Not "Product" or "Feature" Team?

In the past, many software-delivery frameworks used the terms "product team" or "feature team" to refer to teams with a remit to deliver valuable end-to-end software increments, but these days there are many reasons why talking about streams makes more sense than talking about products or features. Aligning a team's purpose with a stream helps to reinforce a focus on flow at the organization level—a stream should flow unimpeded.

With the advent of IoT, embedded devices everywhere, and holistic approaches to service management, the end-to-end user experience looks different. Customers interact not just with a discrete piece of software but with a range of products and devices that all run different kinds of software, from mobile to embedded to voice-led controls. Customers also interact with brands via multiple channels (in person, social media, website, phone), expecting consistent responses and interfaces. In the book *Designing Delivery*, Jeff Sussna talks about the need for teams to include "continuous design" capabilities to meet these challenges: with continuous design we "treat ideas such as service, feedback, failure, and learning as first-class concepts," and the best way to enable this is with a stream-oriented view of change with an emphasis on flow.[6]

In this multi-channel, highly connected context, a "product" can mean very different things, making it hard to understand what the responsibilities of a "product team" are. For instance, in manufacturing companies, the product might be a fixed-life physical device built by an engineering team for a number of years and then disbanded as the product is superseded.

Not only is the term "stream aligned" more suited to a wider range of situations than either "product" of "feature," but "stream aligned" also incorporates and helps to emphasize a sense of flow (because a stream flows). Finally, not all software situations need products or features (especially those focused on providing public services), but all software situations benefit from alignment to flow.

Expected Behaviors

As we've seen, the mission of stream-aligned teams is to ensure the smooth flow of work for a given stream, often related to a business domain area but not always.

What kind of behaviors and outcomes do we expect to see in an effective stream-aligned team?

- A stream-aligned team aims to produce a steady flow of feature delivery.
- A stream-aligned team is quick to course correct based on feedback from the latest changes.
- A stream-aligned team uses an experimental approach to product evolution, expecting to constantly learn and adapt.
- A stream-aligned team has minimal (ideally zero) hand-offs of work to other teams.
- A stream-aligned team is evaluated on the sustainable flow of change it produces (together with some supporting technical and team-health metrics).

- A stream-aligned team must have time and space to address code quality changes (sometimes called "tech debt") to ensure that changing the code remains safe and easy to do.
- A stream-aligned team proactively and regularly reaches out to the supporting fundamental-topologies teams (complicated subsystem, enabling, and platform).
- Members of a stream-aligned team feel they have achieved or are in the path to achieving "autonomy, mastery, and purpose," the three key components of engaged knowledge workers, according to Daniel Pink.[7]

(We will provide a more detailed view of how stream-aligned teams relate to the platform in Chapter 8.)

Enabling Teams

In the book *Accelerate*, Forsgren, Humble, and Kim tell us that high-performing teams are continuously improving their capabilities in order to stay ahead. But how can a stream-aligned team with end-to-end ownership find the space for researching, reading about, learning, and practicing new skills? Stream-aligned teams are also under constant pressure to deliver and respond to change quickly.

An enabling team is composed of specialists in a given technical (or product) domain, and they help bridge this capability gap. Such teams cross-cut to the stream-aligned teams and have the required bandwidth to research, try out options, and make informed suggestions on adequate tooling, practices, frameworks, and any of the ecosystem choices around the application stack. This allows the stream-aligned team the time to acquire and evolve capabilities without having to invest the associated effort (in our experience, such efforts and their impact on the rest of the team also tend to be dramatically underestimated by ten to fifteenfold).

Enabling teams have a strongly collaborative nature; they thrive to understand the problems and shortcomings of stream-aligned teams in order to provide effective guidance. Jutta Eckstein calls them "Technical Consulting Teams,"[8] a definition that maps well to what we'd expect a consulting team to provide (guidance, not execution), whether internal or external to the organization.

Enabling teams actively avoid becoming "ivory towers" of knowledge, dictating technical choices for other teams to follow, while helping teams to understand and comply with organization-wide technology constraints. This is akin to the idea of "servant leadership" but applied to team interactions rather than individuals. The end goal of an enabling team is to increase the autonomy of stream-aligned teams by growing their capabilities with a focus on their problems first, not the solutions per se. If an enabling team does its job well, the team that it is helping should no longer need the help from the enabling team after a few weeks or months; there should not be a permanent dependency on an enabling team.

> **TIP**
>
> Use these heuristics from Robert Greenleaf to guide the behavior and drive of the enabling team: "Do those served grow as persons? Do they, while being served, become healthier, wiser, freer, more autonomous?"[9]

A single enabling team might map to any of the stream-aligned team capabilities we listed in the previous section (user experience, architecture, testing, and so on), but often they are focused on more specific areas, such as build engineering, continuous delivery, deployments, or test automation for particular client technology (e.g., desktop, mobile, web). For example, the enabling team might set up a walking skeleton of a deployment pipeline or a basic test framework combining automation tools and some initial scenarios and examples.

Knowledge transfer between an enabling and a stream-aligned team can take shape on a temporary basis (when a stream-aligned team adopts a new technology, like containerization, for instance) or on a long-term basis (for continuously improving aspects, such as faster builds or faster test execution). Pairing can be quite effective for some types of practices, such as defining Infrastructure-as-Code.

Expected Behaviors

As we've seen, the mission of enabling teams is to help stream-aligned teams acquire missing capabilities, usually around a specific technical or product management area.

What kind of behaviors and outcomes do we expect to see in an effective enabling team?

- An enabling team proactively seeks to understand the needs of stream-aligned teams, establishing regular checkpoints and jointly agreeing when more collaboration is needed.
- An enabling team stays ahead of the curve in keeping abreast of new approaches, tooling, and practices in their area of expertise, well before an actual need is expected from stream-aligned teams. In the past, this has been the mission of architecture or innovation teams, but the focus on enabling other teams creates a better dynamic.
- An enabling team acts as a messenger of both good news (e.g., "There's a new UI automation framework that can reduce our custom test code by 50%.") and bad news (e.g., "Javascript framework X, which we're using extensively, is no longer actively maintained."). This helps with management of the technology life cycle.
- Occasionally, the enabling team might act as a proxy for external (or internal) services that are currently too difficult for stream-aligned teams to use directly.
- An enabling team promotes learning not only inside the enabling team but across stream-aligned teams, acting as a curator that facilitates appropriate knowledge sharing inside the organization (supporting what Tom DeMarco and Tim Lister call a "key learning function."[10]

CASE STUDY: ENGINEERING ENABLEMENT TEAM WITHIN A LARGE LEGAL ORGANIZATION

Robin Weston, Engineering Leader, BCG Digital Ventures

In 2017, I led a year-long consulting engagement with a newly-formed engineering enablement team within a large legal organization. The organization's software development capability was spread among multiple global teams.

The engineering enablement team was formed in response to a number of painful symptoms being felt throughout the organization, such as including long feature lead times, coupled release cycles for separate systems, low team morale, siloed technical knowledge, and (most fundamentally) the organization losing ground to competitors due to the inability to keep up an innovative pace of change.

The enablement team consisted of a number of people with strong skills and awareness across software engineering disciplines (application development, build and release, testing, etc.). Crucially, rather than just bringing in new technology and tools, we focused on sharing good practices and educating teams. Introducing new build and deployment tooling without tackling the underlying culture and development teams' skills can actually do more harm than good. We devised and published a "team charter" that we committed to and shared openly throughout the organization:

Our high-level goal is to enable teams to deliver features faster and with higher quality. We have an initial eight weeks to improve the following metrics:

- Time taken per successful deployment
- Absolute number of successful deployments per day
- Time taken to fix a failing deployment
- Time from code commit to deployment (cycle time)

Trying to fix engineering issues by mandating them from above is doomed to failure, as you really need buy-in from the folks working at the coalface. The enablement team itself was intentionally formed from a mix of external consultants and developers taken from the existing teams. To help launch the team and its mission, we ran an organization-wide workshop, inviting representatives from all global development teams.

I felt strongly that an engineering enablement team should plan for its own extinction from the very first day to avoid other teams becoming dependent. We broadcasted all the work that we were doing with the aim that all other teams would become self-sufficient. To this end, we ran mob programming sessions, recorded demos, and invited every team to our showcases. We estimated that a quarter of our team's time was spent actually implementing solutions; the rest was sharing knowledge.

After the first eight weeks, we saw the following results from our key metrics:

- 72% decrease in deployment lead time
- 700% increase in deployment pipeline runs per day

- Deployment pipeline run duration decreased 98% (from ten hours down to fifteen minutes!)
- Failing build fixed within twenty-three hours on average (previously there had never been a green build!)

Although the absolute numbers themselves weren't that impressive, the fact that we could demonstrate clear progress was a great confidence boost and gave us the trust within the organization to push for more wide-reaching changes to attack other pain points.

The primary purpose of an enabling team is to help stream-aligned teams deliver working software in a sustainable, responsible way. Enabling teams do not exist to fix problems that arise from poor practices, poor prioritization choices, or poor code quality within stream-aligned teams. Stream-aligned teams should expect to work with enabling teams only for short periods of time (weeks or months) in order to increase their capabilities around a new technology, concept, or approach. After the new skills and understanding have been embedded in the stream-aligned team, the enabling team will stop daily interaction with the stream-aligned team, switching their focus to a different team.

Enabling Team versus Communities of Practice (CoP)

Both enabling teams and communities of practice (CoP) can help to increase awareness and capabilities within other teams. The members of an enabling team work on enabling activities full-time, whereas a CoP is a more diffuse grouping of interested individuals from across several teams, with an aim to share practices and improve working methods on a weekly (or monthly) basis. In her book *Building Successful Communities of Practice*, Emily Webber says "Communities of practice create the right environment for social learning, experiential learning, and a rounded curriculum, leading to accelerated learning for members."[11]

Enabling teams and CoP can co-exist because they have slightly different purposes and dynamics: an enabling team is a small, long-lived group of specialists focused on building awareness and capability for a single team (or a small number of teams) at any one point in time, whereas a CoP usually seeks to have more widespread effects, diffusing knowledge across many teams. Of course, several enabling teams can also have their own "enabling-teams community of practice!"

Complicated-Subsystem Teams

A complicated-subsystem team is responsible for building and maintaining a part of the system that depends heavily on specialist knowledge, to the extent that most team members must be specialists in that area of knowledge in order to understand and make changes to the subsystem.

The goal of this team is to reduce the cognitive load of stream-aligned teams working on systems that include or use the complicated subsystem. The team handles the subsystem complexity via specific capabilities and expertise that are typically hard to find or grow. We can't expect to embed the necessary specialists in all the stream-aligned teams that make use of the subsystem; it would not be feasible, cost-effective, or in line with the stream-aligned team's goals.

Examples of complicated subsystems might include a video processing codec, a mathematical model, a real-time trade reconciliation algorithm, a transaction reporting system for financial services, or a face-recognition engine.

The critical difference between a traditional component team (created when a subsystem is identified as being or expected to be shared by multiple systems) and a complicated-subsystem team is that the complicated-subsystem team is created only when a subsystem needs mostly specialized knowledge. The decision is driven by team cognitive load, not by a perceived opportunity to share the component.

Consequently, we expect to have only a few complicated-subsystem teams in a Team Topologies–driven organization when compared to the number of component teams in a traditional structure. (Later in this chapter, we'll look at how to map traditional component teams to one of the fundamental topologies supporting stream-aligned teams.)

Expected Behaviors

As we've seen, the mission of complicated-subsystem teams is to off-load work from stream-aligned teams on particularly complicated subsystems that need to be developed by a group of specialists.

What kind of behaviors and outcomes do we expect to see in an effective complicated-subsystem team?

- A complicated-subsystem team is mindful of the current stage of development of the subsystem and acts accordingly: high collaboration with stream-aligned teams during early exploration and development phases; reduced interaction and focus on the subsystem interface and feature evolution and usage during later stages, when the subsystem has stabilized.

- With a complicated-subsystem team, delivery speed and quality for the subsystem is clearly higher than if/when the subsystem was being developed by a stream-aligned team (before the decision to split).
- The complicated-subsystem team correctly prioritizes and delivers upcoming work respecting the needs of the stream-aligned teams that use the complicated subsystem.

Platform Teams

The purpose of a platform team is to enable stream-aligned teams to deliver work with substantial autonomy. The stream-aligned team maintains full ownership of building, running, and fixing their application in production. The platform team provides internal services to reduce the cognitive load that would be required from stream-aligned teams to develop these underlying services.

This definition of "platform" is aligned with Evan Bottcher's definition of a digital platform:

> A digital platform is a foundation of self-service APIs, tools, services, knowledge and support which are arranged as a compelling internal product. Autonomous delivery teams can make use of the platform to deliver product features at a higher pace, with reduced coordination.[12]

This approach has been successfully adopted in many internet-era organizations. The platform team's knowledge is best made available via self-service capabilities via a web portal and/or programmable API (as opposed to lengthy instruction manuals) that the stream-aligned teams can easily consume. "Ease of use" is fundamental for platform adoption and reflects the fact that platform teams must treat the services they offer as products that are reliable, usable, and fit for purpose, regardless of if they are consumed by internal or external customers. Jutta Eckstein has a suitable recommendation: "Technical-service teams should always regard themselves as pure service providers for the domain teams."[13]

Peter Neumark, former platform engineer at Prezi, stresses the need for alignment of purpose between the platform team and the stream-aligned teams they support: "A platform team's value can be measured by the value of the services they provide to product teams."[14]

In practice, platform teams are expected to focus on providing a smaller number of services of acceptable quality rather than a large number of services with many resilience and quality problems. There will always be a need to balance the effort invested with quality. As with commercial products, the platform can provide different levels of service. If all the stream-aligned teams ask for "premium level" services (e.g., zero downtime of the service, auto scaling, self-recovery in case of failure), then it will likely become impossible for the platform team to cope with demand.

> **TIP**
>
> Don Reinertsen recommends using internal pricing (for infrastructure and services) to regulate demand, helping to avoid everyone asking for premium level.[15] An example could be tracking cloud-infrastructure costs by team or service.

There is a wide range of boundaries for what a platform can be. A thick platform might consist of the combination of several inner platform teams providing a myriad of services. A thin platform could simply be a layer on top of a vendor-provided solution. (Later in this chapter, we expand on what constitutes a good platform.)

Platform examples at a lower level of the stack could range from provisioning a new server instance to providing tools for access management and security enforcement. A stream-aligned team can then decide to use these patterns without fearing a lack of in-depth skills or effort available to acquire them.

> **NOTE**
>
> Common platforms we find abstract away infrastructure, networking, and other cross-cutting capabilities at a lower level of the stack. This is a great first step but, as explained later in this chapter, a platform can refer to a higher level of abstraction.

Expected Behaviors

As we've seen, the mission for a platform team is to provide the underlying internal services required by stream-aligned teams to deliver higher level services or functionalities, thus reducing their cognitive load.

What kind of behaviors and outcomes do we expect to see in an effective platform team?

- A platform team uses strong collaboration with stream-aligned teams to understand their needs.
- A platform team relies on fast prototyping techniques and involves stream-aligned team members for fast feedback on what works and what does not.
- A platform team has a strong focus on usability and reliability for their services (treating the platform as a product), and regularly assesses if the services are still fit for purpose and usable.
- A platform team leads by example: using the services they provide internally (when applicable), partnering with stream-aligned teams and enabling teams, and consuming lower level platforms (owned by other platform teams) whenever possible.
- A platform team understands that adoption of internal new services, like new technologies, is not immediate, but instead evolves along an adoption curve.

CASE STUDY: SKY BETTING & GAMING—PLATFORM FEATURE TEAMS (PART 1)

Michael Maibaum, Chief Architect, Sky Betting & Gaming

Sky Betting & Gaming is a British-based gambling company owned by The Stars Group, with headquarters in Leeds, West Yorkshire, and offices in Sheffield, London, Guernsey, Rome, and Germany. Founded in 1999, the company has been a major force for innovation in the online betting and gaming industry. From around 2009, the company began investing heavily in in-house technical expertise in order to drive rapid innovation, effective delivery, and 24/7 operations.

Since I joined the company in 2012, Sky Betting & Gaming (SB&G) has been a place of almost constant, rapid change. To begin with, technology at SB&G was an infrastructure focused function, focused on hosting applications developed by third parties. In 2009, after a period of relatively slow growth, the business decided it needed to be able to move faster and have more control.

Our in-house software delivery has always taken an Agile approach; as it grew, we went through a number of organizational changes, moving from a small number of scrum teams to many squads in tribes and subtribes. Early in that process, we started incorporating DevOps into the way we worked. We started with specific goals in mind and a distinct "seed" team—for example, improving build and release tools, because while we were successfully being "Agile" in our software development, we realized we were having problems delivering it to live efficiently and reliably. Later, we used DevOps practices as a core part of squads, and eventually we evolved dedicated reliability teams, combined with operations people being embedded in the delivery teams.

During this time of rapid growth, we needed to solve the problem of configuration management, and to make our services more reliable and to help provide the tools needed to maintain a disaster recovery (DR) environment in sync with production systems. Drawing from the lessons of how we started our DevOps journey, we created a platform evolution team drawn from a mixture of software and infrastructure backgrounds. The platform evolution team's first priority was implementing a configuration management system using the well-known tool Chef—working to "Chef all the things," working through the backlog of existing systems, and trying to support the rollout of new or changed services.

Soon after this, we started learning some lessons pretty quickly. The initial implementation of Chef at SB&G was the product of a centralized function with a specific goal (help fix DR), battling to keep up with a period of rapid change and expansion. It became clear that this organizational origin had resulted in a design approach that became a significant constraint. We had a large Chef environment and a significant set of tools built up around it for platform control that lots of people used. Soon they started tripping over each other—problems with shared dependencies, differing priorities, difficulties upgrading—all the usual problems of coupled systems shared between many teams.

(Continued in Chapter 8)

Compose the Platform from Groups of Other Fundamental Teams

In large organizations, a platform will need more than one team to build and run it (and in some cases, separate streams may each have their own platform). In these situations, a platform is composed of groups of other fundamental team types: stream aligned, enabling, complicated subsystem, and platform. Yes: the platform is itself built on a platform (see more on this later in this chapter). However, the streams to which platform teams align are different from the streams for teams building the main (revenue-generating or customer-facing) products and services. In a platform, the streams relate to services and products within the platform, which could be things like logging and monitoring services, APIs for creating test environments, facilities for querying resource usage, and so on. From the viewpoint of the product owner of the platform, there are clear internal streams of value within the platform to which stream-

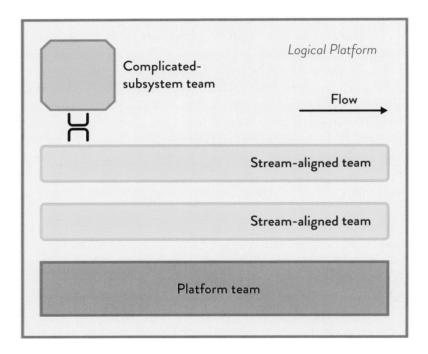

Figure 5.2: Platform Composed of Several Fundamental Team Topologies

In a large organization, the platform is composed of several other fundamental team topologies: stream-aligned Dev teams, complicated-subsystem teams, and a lower-level platform.

aligned teams align to help them deliver value to the customers of the platform: the teams that use the platform (see more on this later in this chapter). We can see these inner topologies in Figure 5.2 on page 96.

In effect, this creates nested or "fractal" teams within the platform—what we like to call inner topologies. As James Womak and Daniel Jones put it, "a product-line manager overseeing an entire product may work with a number of value-stream managers at lower levels taking responsibility for different courses of the value stream."[16] We simply apply the recommendations and guidelines for the various fundamental team topologies *within* the platform boundary.

From the viewpoint of the Dev teams, the platform is a single entity that provides them with a service that they simply consume via an API: machine or container provisioning, network configuration, etc. However, inside the platform team there are several distinct teams (dealing with network, environments, metrics, etc.) that themselves collaborate with or provide a service to other platform teams.

This "nested" approach is similar to the "layered Ops" approach outlined by veteran technologist James Urquhart, based on his experience at Sun Microsystems and Cisco. In the layered approach, one team provides the base infrastructure hardware (physical and virtual) and a second team focuses on running supporting services on top of the base infrastructure.[17] (See Chapter 8 for a more detailed view of this multi-team platform approach.)

CASE STUDY: EVOLVING HIGHLY RESPONSIVE IT OPERATIONS AT AUTO TRADER

Dave Whyte, Operations Engineering Lead, Auto Trader
Andy Humphrey, Head of Customer Operations, Auto Trader

Auto Trader is the UK's largest digital automotive marketplace. It aims to improve the process of buying and selling vehicles in the UK by continually evolving the ecosystem to provide a better experience for consumers, retailers, and manufacturers alike. Auto Trader is a 100% digital business. Starting life as a local classified magazine in 1977, it has grown and evolved alongside its customers. In 2013, it successfully completed the transition from a print title and became a fully digital marketplace. Auto Trader listed on the London Stock Exchange in March 2015 and is now a member of the FTSE 250 Index.

Moving from a print-oriented organization to a 100% digital business required huge changes within Auto Trader. Back in 2013, the organization was very siloed and not joined up, with "the business" in London and "IT" in Manchester, nearly two hundred miles away. IT work was done with big projects—usually with contractors, not permanent staff—and organizational reporting lines caused big problems and mistrust. Developers would leave a project on the day of go-live, which destroyed the sense of operational responsibility and continuity of care for the software systems.

To make things worse, before 2013 new software-development projects were financed with capital expenditure (CapEx) but the IT operations activities were treated as operational expenditure (OpEx,) which produced a sharp divide between teams building things and teams running things. Software development (Dev) time was booked 90% to CapEx; effectively, they were told, "You *must* build new things." They could not work on fixes or things that were right for the customer. Dev was working to serve the "boss" of product management rather than users of the services. We knew we had to change this.

So in 2013, we moved everyone to OpEx. Now everyone is simply doing the work needed to make the company money. With our OpEx-only model, everyone is closer to the customer because we are not thinking about "building new stuff for the product manager" but meeting the needs of users. In fact, OpEx is a deliberate enabling constraint for us: we have a stable workforce of around eight hundred people, and we have no plans to grow hugely. This stable set of people helps with the continuity of care for our software applications and services.

As part of the move to 100% digital, we moved to long-lived, multi-disciplined squads with the responsibility of an end-to-end customer journey. We based the model loosely on the ideas from Spotify but made these work for our context. We also created a special continuous-delivery (CD) team to help other teams adopt CD practices, like automated deployment pipelines, test automation, rich monitoring, and automated environment provisioning. Within three months, we had fully automated deployment for the first application, and then we started on the next application. As this enabling team got more of an understanding of what needed to be done, we realized that it made sense to turn this team into a kind of platform-development team (which we called Infrastructure Engineering).

Fast-forward to 2018, and the remit of Infrastructure Engineering is to build and evolve a platform that takes the pain away from Dev teams, allowing them to take control of their products and services, including operational aspects of their products. Within the platform area, we have several different squads, some focused on new product development for platform features (using standard Agile software development techniques like TDD [test-driven development], retrospectives, and product owners), and some focused on day-to-day operational activities. We don't have any "DevOps" people; instead, we have experienced operations engineers who do in-depth analysis of live service problems. This means that our focus in the infrastructure area is on the flow of work for Dev teams and how application and infrastructure changes affect customers.

The platform enables squads to focus not only on visible product features but also the invisible operational concerns that are essential to a modern digital offering like Auto Trader. The platform gives product squads the time to care about operability. Interestingly, unlike other organizations, we have never embedded Ops people in Dev squads. Instead, we have an Ops "squad buddy" for each Dev squad, a person from Ops who regularly works with specific Dev squads, attending their standups and providing the "glue" between Dev and Ops.

Since 2013, we have had no concept of an IT department within Auto Trader: product and technology are the same department, the same big team. We have taken the Lean thinking approaches of process design and flow into other areas of the organization, so we now have accounts and sales departments using kanban boards with WIP limits. The sales department even does blameless post-incident reviews for missed sales opportunities!

Avoid Team Silos in the Flow of Change

Generally speaking, teams composed only of people with a single functional expertise should be avoided if we want to deliver software rapidly and safely. Traditionally, many organizations created islands, or "silos," of functional expertise by grouping the staff, such as:

- Testing or "quality assurance" (QA)
- Database administration (DBA)

- User experience (UX)
- Architecture
- Data processing (such as ETL)

For years, many organizations used a dedicated "operations" team to manage all aspects of the live or production systems, preventing flow of changes with an explicit hand-off from teams building software coupled with delays accepting the changes. This model also works poorly for safe and rapid flow of change; instead, we combine stream-aligned teams that support and operate software in production together with platform teams that provide the underlying "substrate" for stream-aligned teams.

Organizations that optimize for a safe and rapid flow of change tend to use mixed-discipline or cross-functional teams aligned to the flow of change—what we call stream-aligned teams. Sometimes a particular area is so complicated that a dedicated complicated-subsystem team is needed (see earlier in this chapter). But such teams never sit in the flow of change; instead, they provide services to stream-aligned teams. Work is never handed off to another team for a later stage in the flow.

> **TIP**
>
> **Keeping things simple with cross-functional teams.**
> The use of cross-functional, stream-aligned teams has a very useful side effect. Precisely because stream-aligned teams are composed of people with various skills, there is a strong drive to find the simplest, most user-friendly solution in any given situation. Solutions that require deep expertise in one area are likely to lose against simpler, easier-to-comprehend solutions that work for all members of the stream-aligned team.

A Good Platform Is "Just Big Enough"

A well-designed and well-run platform using what Henrik Kniberg calls "customer-driven platform teams"[18] can be a significant "force multiplier" for software delivery within organizations, but care needs to be taken to ensure that the platform always serves the needs of consuming applications and services, not the other way round.

A good platform provides standards, templates, APIs, and well-proven best practices for Dev teams to use to innovate rapidly and effectively. A good platform should make it easy for Dev teams to do the right things in the right way for the organization; this applies to all kinds of product development, not just those involving software. Too often, a platform is left to former system administrators to build and run without using well-defined software development techniques (Agile practices, TDD, continuous delivery, product management, etc.); or it receives so little funding and attention from the organization that it never helps other teams, only hinders them.

The Thinnest Viable Platform

The simplest platform is purely a list on a wiki page of underlying components or services used by consuming software. If those underlying components and services always work reliably, then there is no need for a full-time platform team. However, as the underlying substrate becomes more complicated—even if all components and services are still outsourced—a platform team can provide a valuable management abstraction over the details of the platform, dealing with the coordination of new and deprecated APIs and components. If an organization needs to build custom solutions and integrations into the platform to meet the needs of Dev teams, then the activities of the platform team increase in scope further.

In all cases, we should aim for a *thinnest viable platform (TVP)* and avoid letting the platform dominate the discourse. As Allan Kelly says, "software developers love building platforms and, without strong product management input, will create a bigger platform than needed."[19] A TVP is a careful balance between keeping the platform small and ensuring that the platform is helping to accelerate and simplify software delivery for teams building on the platform.

Cognitive Load Reduction and Accelerated Product Development

Consider the successful, well-liked software technology platforms of the past few decades: the IBM 8086 processor, the Linux and Windows operating systems, Borland Delphi, the Java Virtual Machine, the .Net Framework, Pivotal Cloud Foundry, Microsoft Azure, and (recently) the IoT platform balena.io and container platform Kubernetes. These platforms have all generally succeeded in reducing the complexity of the underlying systems while exposing enough functionality to be useful to teams building on the platform. This drive to "simplify the developer's life" (as Conway puts it)[20] and reduce cognitive load (see Chapter 3) is an essential aspect of a good platform.

By aiming to reduce cognitive load on Dev teams, a good platform helps Dev teams focus on the germane (differentiating) aspects of a problem, increasing personal and team-level flow, and enabling the whole team to be more effective. As Kenichi Shibata of global publishing company Conde Nast International says, "The most important part of the platform is that it is built for developers."[21]

Compelling, Consistent, Well-Chosen Constraints

To avoid the too-common trap of building a platform disconnected from the needs of teams, it is essential to ensure that the platform teams have a focus on user experience (UX) and particularly developer experience (DevEx). This means that as the platform increases in size, expect to add UX capabilities to the platform teams. Shibata says: "Developers will sometimes have frustrations.... There should be a way to give feedback to platform developers and how the platform is doing in general. Without this, the platform lives in isolation with the rest of the company. Adoption will be strenuous at best."[22]

An attention to good UX/DevEx will make the platform compelling to use, and the platform will feel consistent in the way the APIs and features work. How-to guides and other documentation will be comprehensive (but not verbose), up to date, and focused on achieving specific tasks, not documenting every last corner and niche of the platform.

The platform attempts to "get out of the way" of Dev teams, enabling them to build what they need with few pre-conceptions about how teams need to do that. A good test for DevEx is how easy it is to onboard a new Developer to the platform.

Built On an Underlying Platform

Every software application and every software service is built on a platform. Often the platform is implicit or hidden, or perhaps not noticed much by the team that builds the software, but the platform is still there. As the philosophical expression goes: it's turtles all the way down.

In a software context, this metaphor means that each platform is itself built on another platform, even if the underlying platform is hidden or implied. If the underlying or lower-level platform is not well defined or stable, the upper platform will itself be unstable, and unable to provide the firm foundation needed to accelerate software delivery within the rest of the organization. If the underlying platform has operational quirks or performance problems, the platform team group will need to build insulation abstractions and work-arounds for the operational problems, and/or advertise the potential problems to Dev teams and make it easy for them to avoid hitting the problems. This corresponds with the multi-layer viable-systems model (VSM) described by Stafford Beer in the classic book *Brain of the Firm*.[23]

> **TIP**
>
> To help clarify the platform layers in use in your organization, draw the platform layers on a large diagram. This will help to explain to internal platform teams and to teams that use that platform exactly what the platform provides and what it depends on.

Manage as a Live Product or Service

The platform has users (Dev teams) and clearly defined active hours of operation (whenever Dev teams are using it). The users will come to depend on the reliability of the platform and will need an understanding of when new features will appear and when old features will be retired. Therefore, in order to help the Dev team users to be as effective as possible, we need to: (1) treat the platform as a live/production system, with any downtime planned and managed, and (2) use software-product-management and service-management techniques.

When we treat the platform as a live or production system, we need to undertake all the normal activities and practices that we would with any other live system: define the hours of operation, define the response time for incidents and support, ensure we have an on-call rota to support the platform, manage incidents and unplanned downtime with suitable communication channels (such as service status pages), and so on. Naturally, as the platform grows, it can be useful to reconsider exactly what is needed from the teams within the organization and what can actually be provided externally, thereby reducing the need for an ever-increasing operational-support burden on the platform teams: "the platform team's main clientele is the product teams," as Kenichi Shibata says.[24]

So, how do we manage a live software system with well-defined users and hours of operation? By using software-product-management techniques. The platform, therefore, needs a roadmap curated by product-management practitioners, possibly co-created but at least influenced by the needs of users (Dev teams). The platform team will almost certainly be working with user personas for the users (such as Samir the Web Developer, Jennifer the Tester, Mani the Product Owner, Jack the Service Experience Engineer, and so on). The user personas will help the platform team to empathize with the needs, frustrations, and goals of typical users of the platform. Members of the platform teams will engage with customers (Dev teams and others) regularly to understand what they need.

Crucially, the evolution of the platform "product" is not simply driven by feature requests from Dev teams; instead, it is curated and carefully shaped to meet their needs in the longer term. Feature usage is tracked with metrics and used to shape conversations about prioritization. A platform is not just a collection of features that Dev teams happened to ask for at specific points in the past, but a holistic, well-crafted, consistent thing that takes into account the direction of technology change in the industry as a whole and the changing needs of the organization. A good platform will also serve to reduce the need for security and audit teams to spend time with the Dev team.

Convert Common Team Types to the Fundamental Team Topologies

Many organizations would benefit from increasing the clarity around the definition and purpose of their teams. In fact, we think that most organizations would see major gains in effectiveness by mapping each of their teams to one of the four fundamental topologies; that is, identify which of the four fundamental topologies would represent the best way of working for each team, and then change that team's remit to adopt the purpose and behavior patterns of that topology.

Move to Mostly Stream-Aligned Teams for Longevity and Flexibility

Most teams in a flow-optimized organization should be long-lived, multi-disciplined, stream-aligned teams. These teams take ownership of discrete slices of functionality or certain user outcomes, building strong and lasting relationships with business representatives and other delivery teams. Stream-aligned teams can expect to have cognitive load matched to their capabilities through the support and help they get from enabling teams, platform teams, and complicated-subsystem teams.

Infrastructure Teams to Platform Teams

Traditionally, many infrastructure teams were responsible for all aspects of the live/production infrastructure, including any changes to applications deployed on that infrastructure, as shown in Figure 5.3:

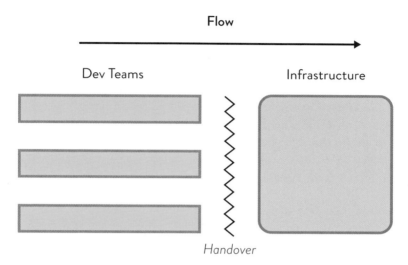

Figure 5.3: Traditional Infrastructure Team Organization
Many traditional infrastructure teams (on the right) blocked flow by being responsible for all changes to production infrastructure, including application changes, frequently gated by ITIL change processes. Work from Dev teams (on the left) was handed over to infrastructure or Ops teams for deployment, preventing flow.

Converting an infrastructure team into a platform team enables rapid, safe flow of change both within the platform and—crucially—within stream-aligned teams.

The change from infrastructure team to platform team is not simple or straightforward, because a platform is managed as a product using proven software development techniques that may be quite unfamiliar to infrastructure people. But as the examples elsewhere in this chapter show, it's an approach that works well.

Component Teams to Platform or Other Team Types

Existing teams based on a technology component should either be dissolved, with the work going into stream-aligned teams or converted into another team type: as part of the platform (if the component is a lower-level "platform" component), to an enabling team (if the component is easy enough for stream-aligned teams to work with), or to a complicated-subsystem team (if the subsystem really is needed and really is too complicated for stream-aligned teams to work with). In any case, the team should adopt the corresponding team behaviors and interaction modes.

For example, database-administrator (DBA) teams can often be converted to enabling teams if they stop doing work at the software-application level and focus on spreading awareness of database performance, monitoring, etc. to stream-aligned teams. Some organizations have had success converting a DBA team into part of the platform, providing a specialized service around database performance, configuration, availability, and so forth, but the DBA team is no longer responsible for schema changes or application-level database concerns.

Likewise, "middleware" teams can also be converted to platform teams if they make those parts of the system easier to use for stream-aligned teams, reducing cognitive load for developers by customizing, simplifying, or wrapping the middleware into easy-to-consume self-serve services aligned to the key organization goals.

Tooling Teams to Enabling Teams or Part of the Platform

A tooling team can easily turn into a siloed tool maintenance team over time if the initial mandate for the team is not specific enough or not time bounded. Besides the emotional attachment to the toolchain, team members' technical skills can become outdated and their effort wasted in minor improvements led by inertia rather than by real needs.

Tooling teams are typically better run either as enabling teams—with a short-lived and highly focused remit—or as part of the platform (with a clear, well-informed roadmap).

Converting Support Teams

Traditionally, many organizations used a single cross-service team to support applications and services in the live/production environments. When speed of change and system complexity were low, this model enabled organizations to optimize costs around the number and skills of people in the support team.

However, with rapid and constant change to software systems, successful organizations are now looking again at the composition and placement of support teams to aid the flow of change rapidly and safely. The model for IT support that consistently seems to work best has two aspects: (1) support

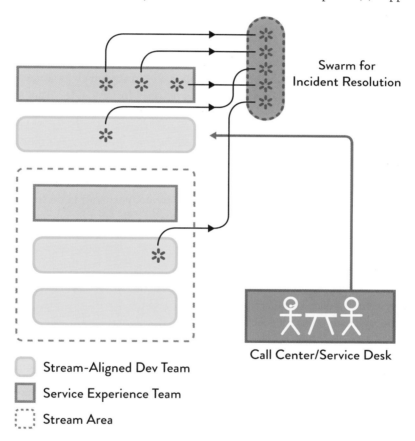

Swarm for
Incident Resolution

Call Center/Service Desk

Stream-Aligned Dev Team

Service Experience Team

Stream Area

Figure 5.4: Support Teams Aligned to Stream of Change
The new model for support teams: aligned to the flow of change,
usually paired with one or more stream-aligned Dev teams.
Incidents are handled with dynamic "swarming."

teams aligned to the stream of changes, and (2) dynamic cross-team activity to resolve live service incidents.

In this model, if dedicated support teams are needed, they are aligned to the stream of change, alongside a team or squad building the software systems. The team with a focus on support sits within the family or tribe of teams that are aligned to the same stream of change. In this context, the team providing support tends to evolve a greater awareness for the experience of the user of the whole service, adding end-to-end synthetic transaction monitoring, particularly in situations where IT and software are only a minor aspect. In fact, some organizations rename such teams "service-experience teams" to take account of the fact that the end-to-end user experience may involve much more than just IT systems, as shown in Figure 5.4 (see page 107).

When an incident occurs with the live production systems, the support teams initially attempt to resolve the problem within stream areas alone. If the problem is entirely within stream, there is no need for any other team to get involved. If necessary, other stream-aligned support teams are brought in to help diagnose the problem; and if the incident affects many teams, a dynamic "swarm" or "incident squad" of support specialists is formed from the various support teams to triage the problem and restore service as rapidly as possible. As service-management specialist Jon Hall explains, there are additional benefits too: the "inclusion of inexperienced frontline support staff in these swarms gives exposure to knowledge that would otherwise only start to be gained after eventual promotion to more specialist teams."[25]

These two different views of support have two important effects: (1) By keeping support teams aligned to streams, we help to keep the streams as independent as possible (as they should be) by creating a strong incentive to design the systems for each stream to be independent at runtime. Effectively, we avoid a Conway's law effect of "monolithization" in the production environment, which otherwise tends to occur with a single team responsible for supporting all production systems. (2) We also rapidly share knowledge of newly discovered limitations and flaws in the software systems, enabling support teams in each stream to feedback learning quickly into teams building the systems.

> **NOTE**
>
> Organizations with a need to interact with users directly over the telephone or in person still maintain a call center or service desk,

> but conceptually, the service desk sits off to one side of the sys-
> tems (away from the flow of change and flow of information from live
> systems), allowing information around live-running systems to flow
> back into the stream-aligned teams.

Converting Architecture and Architects

The most effective pattern for an architecture team is as a part-time enabling team (if one is needed at all). The team being part-time is important: it empha-sizes that many decisions should be taken by implementing teams rather than left to the architecture team. Some organizations compose a virtual team from members of other teams. This virtual team meets regularly to discuss and evolve the architecture aspects of the systems. This is akin to the chapter or guild terminology used by Spotify (see Chapter 4).

Crucially, for effective modern software development, the architecture team should support the other teams, helping them to be as effective as pos-sible, rather than imposing designs or technology choices on other teams. As Forsgren, Humble, and Kim put it in *Accelerate*, "Architects should collaborate closely with their users—the engineers who build and operate the systems through which the organization achieves its mission—to help them achieve better outcomes and provide them the tools and technologies that will enable these outcomes."[26]

A crucial role of a part-time, architecture-focused enabling team is to dis-cover effective APIs between teams and shape the team-to-team interactions with Conway's law in mind. (We cover this aspect of architecture more in Chap-ter 7.)

Summary: Use Loosely Coupled, Modular Groups of Four Specific Team Types

Many organizations struggling with rapid, sustainable software delivery have a wide range of different types of teams, each with different (usually poorly defined) responsibilities. To avoid this problem, restrict teams to just four funda-mental types—stream aligned, enabling, complicated subsystem, and platform. This focuses the organization on team interaction patterns that are known to promote flow at both personal and organizational levels.

Organizations developing and running non-trivial software systems today need to optimize their teams for a safe and rapid flow of change strongly informed by how live production systems work (or fail). This means that the majority of teams need to be loosely coupled, aligned to the flow of change (the "stream"), and capable of delivering a useful increment in the product, service, or user experience for which they are responsible.

Helping stream-aligned teams achieve this high rate of flow are enabling teams (which identify impediments and cross-team challenges, and simplify the adoption of new approaches), complicated-subsystem teams (if needed, to bring deep specialist expertise to specific parts of the system), and platform teams (which provide the underlying "substrate" on which stream-aligned teams can build and support software products and services with minimal friction).

This standardization on the types and responsibilities of teams building and running software systems helps to increase flow by ensuring that most teams are stream aligned, with supporting capabilities and skills provided by enabling, complicated-subsystem, and platform teams.

In turn, the platform itself is run as a product or service, with well-established software-product-management techniques used to prioritize work, regular interaction with customers of the platform (mostly stream-aligned teams), and a strong focus on UX and DevEx. The platform itself may be composed of internal stream-aligned teams, enabling teams, complicated-subsystem teams, and even lower-level platform teams, using the same team types and interactions that are used by the teams consuming the platform.

The focus on empowering stream-aligned teams to achieve fast flow helps to drive decisions at all levels of the organization and provides the overarching mission for all teams.

6 Choose Team-First Boundaries

> When code doesn't work...the problem starts in how teams are organized and [how] people interact.
>
> —**Eric Evans**, *Domain-Driven Design*

Flow is difficult to achieve when each team depends on a complicated web of interactions with many other teams. For a fast flow of change to software systems, we need to remove hand-offs and align most teams to the main streams of change within the organization. However, many organizations experience huge problems with the responsibility boundaries assigned to teams. Typically, little thought is given to the viability of the boundaries for teams, resulting in a lack of ownership, disengagement, and a glacially slow rate of delivery.

In this chapter, we define and explore ways of finding suitable boundaries within and across software systems that enable teams to own and evolve their part of the system effectively and sustainably in ways that encourage flow. These techniques apply equally well to monolithic software and to software that is already more loosely coupled. Crucially, these boundaries are "team sized": we align software and system boundaries to the capabilities of a single team, which immediately makes ownership and sustainable evolution of the software much more feasible.

By carefully exploring and validating the boundaries of responsibility between teams—and using techniques like domain-driven design and fracture planes—we align the software architecture to the problem domain, increasing the flow of changes and providing the organization with the capability to evolve the sociotechnical system more rapidly and effectively.

A Team-First Approach to Software Responsibilities and Boundaries

Many problems in delivering software come from accidentally unclear boundaries between different teams and their responsibilities. This is often shadowed by a software architecture with high coupling between its different parts (even if on paper the architecture was supposed to be highly modular and extensible), as Conway's law tells us. Such a system is commonly called a "monolith."

The research published in *Accelerate* demonstrates that tightly coupled architectures negatively influence the capacity of having autonomous teams with clear responsibilities. The authors also mention architectural approaches that help decouple such architectures: "Architectural approaches that enable this strategy [of supporting teams' full ownership from design through to deployment] include the use of bounded contexts and APIs as a way to decouple large domains into smaller, more loosely coupled units."[1]

But when we want to move from a monolithic software system to more loosely coupled services, we must also consider how the new architecture will affect the teams involved. We need to take into account their cognitive capacity, their location, and their interest in the new services.

Without taking into account the team angle, we risk splitting the monolith in the wrong places or even creating a complex system of interdependent services. This is known as a "distributed monolith" and results in teams lacking autonomy over their services, as almost all changes require updates to other services. Examples like Amazon's service teams (Chapter 4) show that we need to think and guide team interactions to achieve the desired service independence.

Hidden Monoliths and Coupling

There are many kinds of monolithic software, some of which are hard to detect at first. For example, many organizations have taken the time and effort to split up an application monolith into smaller services only to produce a monolithic release further down the deployment pipeline, wasting an opportunity to move faster and safer. We need to be fully aware of what kinds of monoliths we're working with before we start making changes.

Application Monolith

An *application monolith* is a single, large application with many dependencies and responsibilities that possibly exposes many services and/or different user journeys. Such applications are typically deployed as a unit, often causing headaches for users (the application is not available during deployment) and operators (unexpected issues because the production environment is a moving target; even if we tested the monolith in an environment similar to production, it has surely drifted since then).

Joined-at-the-Database Monolith

A *joined-at-the-database monolith* is composed of several applications or services, all coupled to the same database schema, making them difficult to change, test, and deploy separately. This monolith often results from the organization viewing the database, not the services, as the core business engine. It's common to find that one or more database-administration (DBA) teams were put in place to not only maintain the database but also coordinate changes to the database—a task they are often understaffed for—and they become a large bottleneck to delivery.

Monolithic Builds (Rebuild Everything)

A *monolithic build* uses one gigantic continuous-integration (CI) build to get a new version of a component. Application monoliths lead to monolithic builds, but even with smaller services, it's possible that the build scripts set out to build the entire codebase instead of using standard dependency-management mechanisms between components (such as packages or containers).

Monolithic (Coupled) Releases

A *monolithic release* is a set of smaller components bundled together into a "release." When components or services can be built independently in CI but are only able to test in a shared static environment without service mocks, people end up bringing into that same environment all the latest versions of the components. They proceed to deploy the whole set of components as one, as this gives them confidence that what they tested is what will run in production. Sometimes this approach is also the result of having a separate QA team responsible for testing the different components (batching multiple service changes makes sense from the perspective of a QA team with limited capacity).

Monolithic Model (Single View of the World)

A *monolithic model* is software that attempts to force a single domain language and representation (format) across many different contexts. While it may make sense to favor this kind of consistency in small organizations (and only if the teams explicitly agree this is a good idea), this approach can inadvertently start imposing constraints on the architecture and implementation as soon as an organization reaches more than a handful of teams and/or domains.

Monolithic Thinking (Standardization)

Monolithic thinking is "one size fits all" thinking for teams that leads to unnecessary restrictions on technology and implementation approaches between teams. Standardizing everything in order to minimize variation simplifies management oversight of engineering teams, but it comes at a high premium. Good engineers are able and keen to learn new techniques and technologies. Removing teams' freedom to choose by enforcing a single technology stack and/or tooling strongly harms their ability to use the right tool for the job and reduces (or sometimes kills) their motivation. In *Accelerate*, the authors mention how their research indicates that enforcing standardization upon teams actually reduces learning and experimentation, leading to poorer solution choices.[2]

Monolithic Workplace (Open-Plan Office)

A *monolithic workplace* is a single office-layout pattern for all teams and individuals in the same geographic location—typically isolated individual work spaces (cubicles) or an open-plan layout without explicit barriers between people's desks.

The idea that offices should have a standardized layout is prevalent. While it might simplify the work of the building contractor, it can have a recurring negative effect on individuals and teams. Furthermore, the common belief that open-plan offices increase collaboration has been disputed by a field study that found that in two organizations that adopted open offices "the volume of face-to-face interaction decreased significantly (approximately 70%)... with an associated increase in electronic interaction."[3] In our experience, this happens when there's a misunderstanding that what is needed is colocation of purpose, not just colocation of bodies. (See Chapter 2 for more ideas about team-first office-space layouts, and Chapter 7 for different team-interaction modes.)

Software Boundaries or "Fracture Planes"

Although each kind of monolith brings certain disadvantages, there are also dangers to be aware of when splitting up software between teams. Splitting software can reduce the consistency between different parts of the software and can lead to accidental data duplication across multiple subsystems. The user experience (UX) across multiple parts of the software can be degraded if we're not careful to achieve a coherent UX, and additional complexity can be introduced if we split software into a more distributed system.

First, we must understand what a fracture plane is. A *fracture plane* is a natural seam in the software system that allows the system to be split easily into two or more parts. This splitting of software is particularly useful with monolithic software. The word monolith itself comes from Greek, meaning "single stone." Traditional stonemasons hit stones at particular angles to split the rocks in clean segments, taking advantage of their natural fracture planes. We can look for similar fracture planes in software to find the natural split points that lead to software boundaries.

It is usually best to try to align software boundaries with the different business domain areas. A monolith is problematic enough from a technical standpoint (particularly, the way it slows down the delivery of value over time as building, testing, and fixing issues takes increasingly more time). If that monolith is also powering multiple business domain areas, it becomes a recipe for disaster, affecting prioritization, flow of work, and user experience.

However, there are multiple other possible fracture planes for software, not only business domain areas. We can and should break down a monolith by combining different types of fracture planes.

Fracture Plane: Business Domain Bounded Context

Most of our fracture planes (software responsibility boundaries) should map to business-domain bounded contexts. A *bounded context* is a unit for partitioning a larger domain (or system) model into smaller parts, each of which represents an internally consistent business domain area (the term was introduced in the book *Domain-Driven Design* by Eric Evans[4]).

Martin Fowler explains how a bounded context must have an internally consistent model of the domain area:

> DDD [domain-driven design] is about designing software based on models of the underlying domain. A model acts as a ubiquitous language to

help communication between software developers and domain experts. It also acts as the conceptual foundation for the design of the software itself—how it's broken down into objects or functions. To be effective, a model needs to be unified—that is, to be internally consistent so that there are no contradictions within it.[5]

In the book *Designing Autonomous Teams and Services*, DDD experts Nick Tune and Scott Millett give an example of an online music-streaming service with three subdomains that align well to business areas: media discovery (finding new music), media delivery (streaming to listeners), and licensing (rights management, royalty payments, etc.).[6]

Identifying bounded contexts requires a fair amount of business knowledge and technical expertise, so it's normal to make mistakes initially. But that should not deter you from improving and adapting as you understand your context better, even if that involves some kind of recurring "cost" of service redesign. There is often some level of semantic coupling in our design whereby, in the words of Michael Nygard, "a concept may appear to be atomic just because we have a single word to cover it. Look hard enough and you will find seams where you can fracture that concept."[7] In other words, a piecemeal type of evolution is expected when breaking down systems by bounded context.

Other advantages of applying DDD include focusing on core complexity and opportunities within a bounded context for a given business domain, exploring models via collaboration between business experts (because there are now smaller domains to think about), building software that expresses these models explicitly, and having both business owners and technologists speaking an ubiquitous language within a bounded context.

In summary, the business domain fracture plane aligns technology with business and reduces mismatches in terminology and "lost in translation" issues, improving the flow of changes and reducing rework.

Fracture Plane: Regulatory Compliance

In highly regulated industries, like finance or healthcare, regulatory requirements can often provide hard borders for software. They often require organizations to adopt specific mechanisms for auditing, documenting, testing, and deploying software that falls within the scope of those regulations, be it credit card payments, transaction reporting, and so on.

On one hand, it's a good idea to minimize the amount of variation in those processes across different systems. For example, having different release/delivery processes depending on the type of system and changes being made. But ensuring such processes, including manual approvals or activities, are always mapped in the delivery pipeline and having appropriate access controls to the pipeline gives traceability of changes across all systems while covering most auditing requirements.

On the other hand, following strict requirements should not be forced on areas of the system that are not as critical. Splitting off subsystems or flows within the monolith that are in the scope of regulations is a natural fracture plane.

For instance, the Payment Card Industry Data Security Standard (PCI DSS) establishes a set of rules around requesting and storing credit card data. Compliance with PCI DSS should fall on a dedicated subsystem for card data management, but these requirements should not apply to an entire monolith that happens to *include* payment functionality. Splitting along the regulatory-compliance fracture plane simplifies auditing and compliance, as well as reduces the blast radius of regulatory oversight.

Finally, there's an aspect of team composition and interaction at play here as well, especially in larger organizations. With a single, larger team responsible for the monolith, it's typical that people from compliance and/or legal teams participate only occasionally in planning and prioritization sessions, where the scope of the work does not justify full-time team membership for those stakeholders. When the subsystem gets split off, it suddenly makes more sense to have a smaller but compliance-focused team, including business owners from compliance and/or legal areas.

Fracture Plane: Change Cadence

Another natural fracture plane is where different parts of the system need to change at different frequencies. With a monolith, every piece moves at the speed of the slowest part. If new reporting features are only needed and released on a quarterly basis, then it will likely become very hard, if not impossible, to release other types of features more frequently than that, as the codebase is in flux and not ready for production. Changes get lumped together, and the speed of delivery gets seriously affected.

Splitting off the parts of the system that typically change at different speeds allows them to change more quickly. The business needs now drive the speed of change, rather than the monolith imposing a fixed speed for all.

Fracture Plane: Team Location

Teams distributed geographically and across different time zones are obviously not colocated. But even teams with members working in the same office building on different floors or in different physical spaces can be considered geographically separate.

Within distributed teams, communication is limited since they must explicitly request a physical or virtual space and time to communicate across locations. The remaining (unplanned) intra-team communication (which can be as high as 80%) happens within the physical boundaries of each of the team's partitions.

Working across different time zones aggravates these communication delays and introduces bottlenecks when manual approvals or code reviews are needed from people in different time zones with little working-time overlap. Heidi Helfand stresses the issues with distinct time zones in her book *Dynamic Reteaming*:

> If you must have remote workers, you will need to do extra work to foster the collaboration within the team and between the teams in order to build the community. You should try to have the same time zone versus different time zones; otherwise, people won't want to meet with each other because it cuts into their personal time at home.[8]

We'd argue that for a team to communicate efficiently, the options are between full colocation (all team members sharing the same physical space) or a true remote-first approach (explicitly restricting communication to agreed channels—such as messaging and collaboration apps—that everyone on the team has access to and consults regularly). When neither of these options is feasible (full colocation or remote first), then it's better to split off the monolith into separate subsystems for teams in different locations. In this way, an organization can leverage Conway's law and align the system architecture with the communication constraints in real life.

Fracture Plane: Risk

Different risk profiles might coexist within a large monolith. Taking more risk means accepting a higher probability of system or outcome failure in favor of getting changes into the hands of customers faster. As a side note, having true continuous-delivery capabilities in place with a loosely coupled system architecture (not a monolith) actually decreases the risk of deploying small changes very frequently.

There are multiple types of risks (usually mapped to business appetite for change) that can suggest fracture planes. Regulatory compliance is a specific type of risk, which we addressed earlier. Other examples include marketing-driven changes with a higher risk profile (focusing on customer acquisition) versus lower risk profile changes to revenue-generating transactional features (focusing on customer retention).

The number of users might also drive acceptable risk. For instance, a multi-tier SaaS product might have millions of users in its free tier and only a few hundred customers in the paying tiers. Changes to popular features in the free tier might fall into a higher risk profile, as any major failure could mean losing millions of potential paying customers. Changes to paid-only features might actually sustain less risk if the speed and personalization of support for those few hundred customers makes up for occasional failures. For similar reasons, internal systems in an organization can typically handle higher risk profiles (although that doesn't mean they shouldn't be treated as a regular product, even if they're for internal use only).

Splitting off subsystems with clearly different risk profiles allows mapping the technology changes to business appetite or regulatory needs. It also allows each subsystem to evolve its own risk profile over time, adopting practices like continuous delivery that allow increasing speed of change without incurring more risk.

Fracture Plane: Performance Isolation

In particular types of systems, differentiating levels of performance might be beneficial. Of course, performance should always be a concern for every system; and it should be analyzed, tested, and optimized where possible.

However, parts of applications subject to peaks of demand at a large scale (like yearly tax submissions on the last day), require a level of scaling and failover optimization not necessary for the rest of the system.

Splitting off such a subsystem based on particular performance demands helps to ensure it can scale autonomously, increasing performance and reducing cost. A full tax-return application could then, for example, be composed of a tax submission and validation subsystem that is performance critical and can handle millions of submissions in a short time period. Other subsystems such as tax simulation, processing, and payment can live with less critical performance.

Fracture Plane: Technology

Technology is often (historically) the only type of boundary used when splitting up teams. Consider how common it is to have separate teams for front end, back end, data tier, etc.

However, these common kinds of technology-driven splits typically introduce more constraints and reduce flow of work rather than improve it. That is because the separate teams are less autonomous, as product dependencies remain while each team has less visibility on the work as a whole, and inter-team communication paths are slower than intra-team.

There are situations where splitting off a subsystem based on technology can be effective, particularly for systems integrating older or less automatable technology. Flow can be considerably slower when changes involving such older technology are required, either because more manual tests must be run or difficulties are expecting implementing changes due to poor documentation and lack of an open, supportive community of users (a given for modern tech stacks). Finally, the ecosystem of tools (IDEs, build tools, testing tools, etc.) around such technology tends to behave and feel very different from modern ecosystems, increasing the cognitive load on team members that need to switch between these very different technologies. Splitting the team responsibilities along technology lines in these cases can help teams to own and evolve software effectively.

When deciding whether to split along technology fracture planes, first investigate whether alternative approaches could help increase the pace of change in older tech, as that would remove constraints and benefit the business (while allowing a monolith split along more valuable fracture planes, like business-aligned bounded contexts). For example, in his book *DevOps for the Modern Enterprise*, Mirco Hering explains how to apply good coding and version-control practices when dealing with proprietary COTS products.[9]

Fracture Plane: User Personas

As systems grow and expand their feature sets, their customer base (internal or external) also grows and diversifies. Some groups of users will rely on a given subset of features to get their jobs done, while other groups will require another subset. In products with tiered pricing, the subset is built in by design (higher paying customers have access to more features than lower or non-paying customers). In other systems, admin users have access to more options and controls than regular users; or simply, more experienced users make more use of certain features (like keyboard shortcuts) than novice users. Thus, it makes sense to split off subsystems for user personas in these types of situations.

The effort required to remove dependencies or coupling between features is compensated with a sharper focus on customers' needs and experience using the system, which should result in higher customer satisfaction and improve the organization's bottom line. In fact, such a structure can also improve the speed and quality of customer support—it becomes easier to map issues to a given subsystem and team. Teams responsible for subsystems aligned with enterprise personas might want to ensure there is always availability to deal with (enterprise) support issues as smoothly as possible.

Natural "Fracture Planes" for Your Specific Organization or Technologies

Sometimes other natural or available team-first fracture planes for assigning work can be identified. The litmus test for the applicability of a fracture plane: Does the resulting architecture support more autonomous teams (less dependent teams) with reduced cognitive load (less disparate responsibilities)?

Of course, achieving such results often requires some initial experimentation and fine tuning. It is unlikely to guarantee a specific end result without actually giving it a fair try first. A simple heuristic that can help guide assessment of your system and team boundaries is simply to ask: Could we, as a team, effectively consume or provide this subsystem as a service? If the answer is yes, then the subsystem is a good candidate for splitting off and assigning to a team to own and evolve.

FINDING GOOD SOFTWARE BOUNDARIES AT POPPULO

Stephanie Sheehan, VP of Operations at Poppulo
Damien Daly, Director of Engineering at Poppulo

Poppulo enables organizations to plan, target, publish, and measure the impact of their communications across multiple digital channels, all in one place. Over four years from 2012 we trebled in size, opened offices in the US, and grew an extensive customer portfolio of the world's greatest brands, including Nestlé, Experian, LinkedIn, Honda, and Rolls-Royce. As of 2019, the Poppulo platform is used by more than 15 million employees in more than a hundred countries. Getting to this point we have had to scale from a single development team to eight product teams, one SRE team, and an infra-team in the space of three years.

Back in 2015, we expected significant growth in our customer base and in the size of our engineering staff, so we wanted to make sure that we split up the monolith in a way that helped the new teams to be largely independent and autonomous. As we hired more engineers, the architecture and practices which worked for a single team were not going to scale. We put DevOps and continuous delivery practices at the center of our design choices and started transitioning to a microservices-type architecture from our existing (successful) monolithic system.

We began by adopting a stronger focus on "the team" as the means to get work done. Previously we sometimes had bottlenecks around individuals, but by taking a team approach and adopting practices like pairing (and later, mobbing) we began to see better flow of work as team members helped each other to complete tasks. We then began instrumenting our code and adding telemetry so that we had visibility of how the code actually worked in production. Together with end-to-end deployment pipelines, the improved logging and metrics allowed teams to understand the code better and start to take ownership.

The Poppulo products help organizations to communicate electronically with large numbers of people, so our business domains are centered around concepts like people, content, events, email, mobile, and analytics. We knew from reading and watching conference talks the importance of giving aligned autonomy to delivery teams through clean separation of domains. We therefore spent some time assessing how independent each domain really was and playing though scenarios on whiteboards before splitting the software along these domain boundaries. We were keen to ensure that we were not too adversely affected by Conway's law, so making sure that we had effective domain separation was crucial.

We value collaboration and autonomy in our work, so we organized ourselves into "matrix product teams," cross functional teams who sit together and completely own an area of the product. Our product teams are typically made up of four developers, one production manager, one QA, and one UX/UI designer. Our teams speak directly to customers and stakeholders: they shadow support calls; they design, build, and measure the impact of their solutions; and they are accountable for the quality of the solutions they deliver.

We use some techniques from DDD, particularly event storming, to understand and model the domains in our business context. At a more technical level, we use Pact for contract testing services and inter-team communication. Pact has really helped us to adopt a clear, defined approach to testing services, setting expectations across all teams about how to test and interact with other teams.

Most of our delivery teams are aligned to business domain bounded contexts such as email, calendar, people, surveys, and so on. We also have a few parts of the system that align to regulatory boundaries (particularly ISO 27001 for information security management) and to the need for cross-domain reporting of feature usage. These areas are handled by either a small specialist team or through collaboration across several teams.

We also have a team that helps to provide consistent user experience (UX) across all parts of the software. The UX team acts as internal consultants across all the delivery teams, enabling them to adopt good UX practices quickly. We run an SRE capability for dealing with the high volume of traffic and enhancing operability.

Taking the time to understand our business domains and split our monolithic software up to match the domains has helped us to scale our engineering division from sixteen people to seventy people since 2015. Investing in telemetry and a good operational focus has helped the teams understand the software they are building. By adopting cross-functional product teams with what we call "aligned autonomy" we have seen good ownership of software services within teams, which in turn enables us to have a fast flow of change while minimizing downtime.

Real-World Example: Manufacturing

When we talked about technology as a fracture plane, we stressed how this should be applied sparsely and mostly for older technology that feels and behaves considerably different from modern software stacks. Inevitably, you will find exceptions. The difficulty is understanding when an exception is valid and when an easy way to make quick progress ultimately limits effectiveness.

To illustrate, let's look at a scenario that we found at a rather large manufacturing client we worked for. This large manufacturing company produces physical devices for consumers. All the devices are equipped with IoT capabilities,

Cloud as Platform

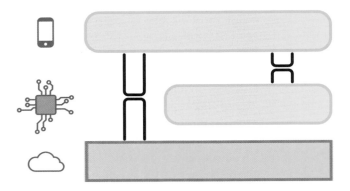

Embedded IoT Device as Platform

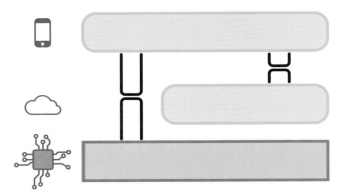

Figure 6.1: Mobile, Cloud, and IoT Technology Fracture Plane Scenario
With three very disparate technologies (mobile, cloud, and IoT), an organization must
decide on an approach to fracture planes that makes sense based on
the cognitive load and the change cadence in each area.

including remote control from a mobile app and remote software updates via the
cloud. Devices are controlled from both the cloud (via scheduled activity) and by
interactive user control (using the mobile app). All activity logs and product data
are sent to the cloud, where they are processed, filtered, and stored.

It would be extremely challenging for a stream-aligned team to own this
entire end-to-end user experience—mobile app, cloud processing, and embedded software for the device—given the size and cognitive-load limitations

highlighted early in the book. Making end-to-end changes across three very different tech stacks (embedded, cloud, and mobile) requires a skill mix that is hard to find, and the associated cognitive load and context switching would be untenable. At best, changes would be suboptimal in technical and architectural terms; at worst, they would be fragile, lead to steadily increasing technical debt, and possibly provide a poor user experience for customers overall.

Instead, by accepting the technical limitations of the system, teams could be organized along the natural technology boundaries (an embedded team, a cloud team, and possibly, a mobile team). The gap between these technologies (in terms of skills and speed of deployment) imposes a different pace of change for each, which is the key driver for separate teams.

There are two main options in this case (see Figure 6.1 on page 124): (1) Treat the cloud software as the platform and the mobile and embedded IoT software as clients/consumers of the platform. This will work well if the rate or ease of change of the consuming apps is at least as rapid as changes in the cloud platform. (2) Treat the embedded IoT devices as a platform and make the cloud and mobile apps clients/consumers of this platform. Either model can work, but in each, the team behaving as a platform will need to adopt platform-like approaches.

This approach will require regular coordination between teams for features that impact two or more technology areas. Changes might need to be scheduled to the cloud platform's APIs before a new software version can be deployed to the embedded devices. This coordination, however, should also serve to establish common ways of working between the teams (e.g., semantic versioning, logging approaches, API-first development).

Over time, these shared practices and knowledge might enable a future restructure of team boundaries, as the pace of change becomes more similar across technologies.

Summary: Choose Software Boundaries to Match Team Cognitive Load

When optimizing for flow, stream-aligned teams should be responsible for a single domain. This is a challenge when domains are hidden in monolithic systems that include many different responsibilities and are mostly driven by technology choices, providing functionalities across multiple areas of business.

We need to look for natural ways to break down the system (fracture planes) that allow the resulting parts to evolve as independently as possible.

Consequently, teams assigned to those parts will experience more autonomy and ownership over them.

Looking to align subsystem boundaries with (mostly independent) segments of the business is a great approach, and the domain-driven design methodology supports that approach nicely. But we need to beware and sense for other fracture planes, such as change cadence, risk, regulatory compliance, and so on. Often, a combination of fracture planes will be required.

Finally, we need to be aware of different types of monoliths impeding flow and causing unnecessary dependencies between teams. While we typically think of system architecture as a monolith, there are other, more subtle ways in which coupling creeps in, even when the system architecture is already modular (for example, shared databases, coupled builds and/or releases, and more). As Amy Phillips puts it, "If you have microservices but you wait and do end-to-end testing of a combination of them before a release, what you have is a distributed monolith."[10]

When considering subsystem boundaries, the main aim should be to find software fracture planes that align to business domain bounded contexts, because most of these bounded contexts will map to streams of change that are natural for the organization. This, in turn, means that business-domain boundaries can be aligned to stream-aligned teams, helping to focus on flow across the organization.

Fracture planes can be chosen around specific challenges (e.g., technology, regulation, performance, geographic location of staff, user personas) to help avoid hand-offs between teams and promote flow.

In all cases, it is essential to make software segments team sized so that teams can effectively own and evolve their software in a sustainable way.

PART III
Evolving Team Interactions for Innovation and Rapid Delivery

KEY TAKEAWAYS

CHAPTER 7

- Choose specific team interaction modes to enhance software delivery.
- Choose between three team interaction modes—collaboration, X-as-a-Service, and facilitating—to help teams provide and evolve services to other teams.
- Collaboration can be a powerful driver for innovation but can also reduce flow.
- X-as-a-Service can help other teams deliver quickly but only if the boundary is suitable.
- Facilitating helps to avoid cross-team challenges and detects problems.

CHAPTER 8

- Use different team topologies simultaneously for strategic advantage.
- Change team topologies and team interactions to accelerate adoption of new approaches.
- Differentiate between explore, exploit, sustain, retire phases using team topologies.
- Expect multiple, simultaneous team topologies to meet different needs.
- Recognize triggers for organization change.
- Treat operations as high-fidelity sensory input for self-steering.

CONCLUSION

- Combine a team-first approach with Conway's law, the four fundamental topologies, team interaction modes, topology evolution, and organizational sensing.
- Get started: begin with the team, identify streams, identify the thinnest viable platform, identify capability gaps, and practice team interactions.

7

Team Interaction Modes

Technologies and organizations should be redesigned to intermittently isolate people from each other's work for best collective performance in solving complex problems.
—Ethan Bernstein, Jesse Shore, and David Lazer,
"How Intermittent Breaks in Interaction Improve
Collective Intelligence"

I n Part II, we saw how combinations of the four fundamental team topologies—stream aligned, enabling, complicated subsystem, and platform—provide a clear pattern for software delivery with fast flow. However, simply arranging teams into patterns is not enough for high effectiveness; it is also necessary to identify how these teams interact and when to change the teams and their interactions.

Part III will look at how the evolution of team interactions can become a strategic advantage for organizations building software systems. Through a combination of well-defined team interaction patterns and clear heuristics for evolving team topologies, organizations can use team interactions as a sensing mechanism for innovation and self-steering toward better customer or user outcomes.

So far, we have seen several static (point-in-time) team topologies that work well for different scenarios, along with some guidelines for choosing sensible team boundaries. However, it is not sufficient to simply choose a team boundary a single time and expect no further changes; instead, organizations must anticipate the need for evolution of team patterns to meet business, organizational, market, technological, and personnel needs.

As teams gain more experience.in one area, new technology becomes available, or the organization expands and contracts in size, the dynamics between teams and economics (particularly the economies of scale) change, and the choice of team topologies can help facilitate that change. In some cases, the same two teams might need to collaborate closely at some point in time but be independent six or nine months later in order to achieve the most effective software delivery outcomes. The team topologies used should adapt and evolve to meet emerging challenges, while still retaining the key team-focused and architectural considerations encountered in Part I.

In this chapter, we explore three core *team interaction modes* that simplify and clarify the essential interactions needed between teams building software systems: *collaboration*, *X-as-a-Service*, and *facilitating*. These team interaction modes define expectations and behavior patterns for all teams in the organization, simplifying team interactions and acting as a way to detect misaligned boundaries.

We will also explore some essential team interaction modes that should guide choice of evolution for team topologies. The dynamics behind team interaction modes act as the foundation for choosing team topologies effectively. Crucially, using a well-defined set of team interaction patterns avoids the ambiguity present in many team-software relationships, thereby producing more coherent subsystem boundaries and APIs.

Well-Defined Interactions Are Key to Effective Teams

In many organizations, poorly defined team interactions and responsibilities are a source of friction and ineffectiveness. A team may have been told it is autonomous and self-organizing, but team members find they have to interact with many other teams in order to complete their work; and this feels frustrating. Another team may have responsibility for providing an API or service, but they don't really have the experience to do this effectively.

When considering the relationship between any teams, a key decision is whether to collaborate with another team to achieve an objective or to treat the other team as providing a service (see Figure 7.1 on page 133).This choice between collaboration or consuming a service can be made at many different levels within the organization: consuming infrastructure as a service (from AWS, Azure, or Google Cloud, for instance), collaborating on logging and metrics, relying on a complicated-subsystem team to build a complex audio-processing codec, or working together on application deployment. What must be avoided is the need for all teams to communicate with all other

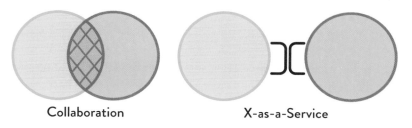

Figure 7.1: Collaboration vs. X-as-a-Service
Collaboration means explicitly working together on defined areas. X-as-a-Service means one team consumes something "as a service" from another team.

teams in order to achieve their ends; just as a jazz band coordinates the music it plays, we should expect to carefully curate the communication that takes place within an organization.

> **NOTE**
>
> **Intermittent collaboration gives the best results.**
> Researchers recently devised an ingenious experiment to assess the effectiveness of team-based solutions to complex problems. Bernstein and colleagues found that "groups whose members interacted only intermittently...had an average quality of solution that was nearly identical to those groups that interacted constantly, yet they preserved enough variation to find some of the best solutions too."[1] Intermittent collaboration found better solutions than constant interaction.

The Three Essential Team Interaction Modes

To understand how and when to adapt the Team Topologies model for software systems, we need to define and understand three essential ways in which teams can and should interact, taking into account team-first dynamics and Conway's law:

- **Collaboration**: working closely together with another team
- **X-as-a-Service**: consuming or providing something with minimal collaboration

- **Facilitating**: helping (or being helped by) another team to clear impediments

A combination of all three team interaction modes is likely needed for most medium-sized and large enterprises (and these modes are useful to introduce at smaller organizations sooner than many people expect). In addition, one team might use two different interaction modes for two different teams with which it works. We represent these different interaction modes graphically using the patterns in Figure 7.2:

Collaboration   X-as-a-Service   Facilitating

Figure 7.2: The Three Team Interaction Modes
Collaboration mode is shown with diagonal cross-hatching, X-as-a-Service
mode is shown with brackets, and facilitating is shown with dots.

For example, let's say Team A is a stream-aligned team working on software for managing personal finances. They may use the collaboration mode to interact with Team B on new cloud-monitoring tooling, and use the X-as-a-Service mode to interact with Team C, which provides the platform on which the software runs (see Figure 7.3 on page 135).

Formalizing the ways in which teams should interact when building software systems helps to more easily assess the effectiveness of many aspects of software delivery by more explicitly defining interfaces between teams; in turn, it is expected (from Conway's law) that these interfaces will be reflected in the software systems being built. Mike Rother, considering the huge success of the Japanese manufacturer Toyota, wrote: "The roots of Toyota's success lie not in its organizational structures but in developing capability and habits in its people."[2]

Interaction modes should become team habits. By expecting and helping to achieve these kinds of team interactions, teams experience increased clarity of purpose, improved team engagement, and reduced frustration with other teams. Limiting team interaction in this way also deliberately addresses the homomorphic aspects of building systems that follow from Conway's law (see Chapter 2). Teams should ask: "What kind of interaction should we have

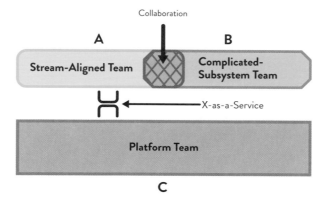

Figure 7.3: Team Interaction Modes Scenario
Stream-aligned Team A collaborates with complicated-subsystem Team B
(shown with cross-hatching) while also consuming the platform provided by Team C,
using the X-as-a-Service mode (shown with brackets).

with this other team? Should we be collaborating closely with the other team? Should we be expecting or providing a service? Or should we be expecting or providing facilitation?"

> **TIP**
>
> A key part of the Team Topologies approach is in the choice between two teams collaborating and one team consuming something "as a service" from another team.

Collaboration: Driver of Innovation and Rapid Discovery but Boundary Blurring

The collaboration team mode is suitable where a high degree of adaptability or discovery is needed, particularly when exploring new technologies or techniques. The collaboration interaction mode is good for rapid discovery of new things, because it avoids costly hand-offs between teams. For instance, perhaps there is significant innovation in a space that spans the expertise of two existing teams, Team A and Team B, such as cloud-based sensor management (combining cloud technologies and sensor technologies) or secure local networking

> Collaboration: working closely together with another team

with wearable devices (combining networking knowledge and expertise from the clothing industry). The collaborative mode requires good alignment and a high appetite and ability for working together between teams.

During early phases of new systems development, and during periods where there is a need to quickly discover new information, technology limitations, and suitable practices, the collaboration mode is highly valuable. This is because team topologies that use collaboration can rapidly uncover new ways of working and unexpected behaviors of technologies.

This collaboration occurs between groups with different skill sets in order to bring together the combined knowledge and experience of many people to solve challenging problems. Collaboration leads to new insights into how technologies work, with learning brought back into other teams (this corresponds to the "divergent thinking" approaches of Dr. Kyung Hee Kim and Robert A. Pierce[3]).

There are two useful ways to visualize teams interacting using the collaboration mode. The first is to visualize two teams with distinct expertise and responsibilities working together on a small set of things. In this first collaboration interaction, the two teams substantially retain their responsibility and expertise for their natural area of focus, and work together on a specific subset of activities and details.

The second visualization of collaboration mode identifies that the nature of working together between teams can be almost total: although there were originally two teams with different skills and expertise, now there is effectively a single team pooling expertise and responsibilities. (Care must be taken to not let the number of people exceed Dunbar's number of fifteen).

In both cases—with a small defined overlap, and with a full overlap of focus and responsibilities—the two teams must take on joint responsibility for the overall outcomes of their collaboration, because the act of collaborating creates a blurring of responsibility boundaries. Without joint responsibility, there is a danger of loss of trust if something goes wrong.

When a team is in the context of discovery or rapid learning that extends beyond the expertise of one team, it should be expected for that team to collaborate closely with another team with different skills. However, the cognitive load of ongoing collaboration can be much higher than working purely inside the team's "natural" area. This means the communication overhead is going to be higher, possibly resulting in the apparent reduction of team effectiveness when viewed as a single team. Instead, the investment in higher effectiveness is being made in the ensemble of the two teams through rapid discovery of new practices.

This, in turn, means that when two teams are interacting using the collaboration mode, there should be a high value gained from working together due to the high cost of collaboration; the reward needs to be tangible. There should also be little or no friction between teams, as any friction will make collaboration difficult.

Furthermore, Conway's law tells us that with the discovery and rapid learning that comes from the collaboration mode, the responsibilities and architecture of the software will tend to be more blended together. If clear, well-defined interfaces to services or systems between two teams is needed, then using the collaboration mode for extended periods is not likely to be the best choice. Short-term or light-touch occasional collaboration to establish or refine the interfaces is fine, but a need for ongoing collaboration suggests incorrect domain boundaries and/or team responsibilities, or the incorrect mix of skills within a team.

Table 7.1: Advantages and Disadvantages of Collaboration Mode

Advantages	Disadvantages
• Rapid innovation and discovery • Fewer hand-offs	• Wide, shared responsibility for each team • More detail/context needed between teams, leading to higher cognitive load • Possible reduced output during collaboration compared to before
Constraint: A team should use collaboration mode with, at most, one other team at a time. A team should not use collaboration with more than one team at the same time.	
Typical Uses: Stream-aligned teams working with complicated-subsystem teams; stream-aligned teams working with platform teams; complicated-subsystem teams working with platform teams	

X-as-a-Service: Clear Responsibilities with Predictable Delivery but Needs Good Product Management

The X-as-a-Service team interaction mode is suited to situations where there is a need for one or more teams to use a code library, component, API, or platform

> X-as-a-Service: consuming
> or providing something
> with minimal collaboration

that "just works" without much effort, where a component or aspect of the system can be effectively provided "as a service" by a distinct team or group of teams.

During later phases of systems development and periods where predictable delivery is needed (rather than discovery of new approaches), the X-as-a-Service model works best. In this model, teams can rely on certain aspects of their technology landscape being provided as a service by other teams (internal or external), allowing the team to focus on delivering their work.

The challenging aspects of the service will already have been discovered by a previous "divergent" approach using close collaboration, leaving the most effective solution to be run as a service. Relying on something "as a service" requires excellent work from the XaaS team(s)—not easy to achieve—but results in the delivery team having to understand less about non-core aspects of their work, allowing them to deliver more quickly (this corresponds to the "divergent thinking" approaches of Dr. Kyung Hee Kim and Robert A .Pierce).

With X-as-a-Service, there is great clarity about who owns what: one team consumes something that the other team provides. Less context is needed by each team compared to working in collaboration mode, so the cognitive load on each side can be "lower than." By design, innovation across the boundary happens more slowly than with collaboration, precisely because X-as-a-Service has a nice, clean API that has defined the service well. We can see this relationship in Figure 7.4.

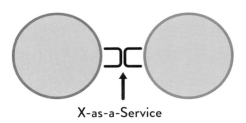

X-as-a-Service

Figure 7.4: X-as-a-Service Team Interaction Mode

In this case, the team on the right is providing something "as a service" to the team on the left (perhaps an API, some developer tooling, or even an entire platform).

For a component or aspect of a system to be provided effectively as a service, not only must the responsibility boundary make sense in the context of the business or technical domain, but the team providing the service will also be required to be adept at understanding the needs of the teams that consume its service and managing their aspect of the system using service-management principles (through the use of versioning, product management, and so forth).

In the X-as-a-Service team interaction mode, the two interacting teams have little need for day-to-day collaboration in order to use or provide the component/API/feature as a service. This is an explicit benefit of the X-as-a-Service model: if the aspect being provided needs little interaction from the consuming team, then—almost by definition—it is highly fit for purpose, and is helping the consuming team to do their work effectively. This means that for the X-as-a-Service model, there should be a high value gained from some teams being able to ignore low-level details of the service that they consume from another team, allowing them to move quickly without needing to be concerned with implementation details.

> **NOTE**
>
> The X-as-a-Service model works well *only* if the service boundary is well chosen and well implemented, with a good service-management practice from the team providing the service.

For something to be provided as a service—whether a component, an API, a testing tool, or an entire delivery platform—the team responsible must have a strong sense of responsibility toward both the consumers and the viability of the thing they are providing. They must make the developer experience (DevEx) highly compelling. The service they provide should be straightforward to use, test, deploy, and/or debug; and the documentation on how to use it should be clear, well-written, and up to date. Furthermore, the service they provide must be managed in a way that keeps it viable over time: requests for new features from consuming teams are considered but not built just because a team has asked for them. Instead, the purpose and remit of the thing is evolved with the best interest of all consumers in mind, with enhancements carefully scheduled and planned in consultation with other teams.

Even a simple code library for, say, low-level XML transformations will benefit from applying product-management and DevEx principles. The team that builds and supports the XML library should think about versioning and backwards compatibility, a communicated roadmap for retiring the older versions of the library, helping consumers of the library move to newer versions, and so on. For anything larger than a code library, the need for these X-as-a-Service approaches is even greater.

Advantages	Disadvantages
· Clarity of ownership with clear responsibility boundaries · Reduced detail/context needed between teams, so cognitive load is limited	· Slower innovation of the boundary or API · Danger of reduced flow if the boundary or API is not effective

Constraint: A team should expect to use the X-as-a-Service interaction with many other teams simultaneously, whether consuming or providing a service.

Typical Uses: Stream-aligned teams and complicated-subsystem teams consuming Platform-as-a-Service from a platform team; stream-aligned teams and complicated-subsystem teams consuming a component or library as a service from a complicated-subsystem team.

Facilitating: Sense and Reduce Gaps in Capabilities

The facilitating team interaction mode is suited to situations where one or more teams would benefit from the active help of another team facilitating (or coaching) some aspect of their work. The facilitating interaction mode is the main operating mode of an enabling team (see Chapter 5) and provides support and capabilities to many other teams, helping to enhance the productivity and effectiveness of these teams. The remit of the team undertaking the facilitation is to enable the other team(s) to be more effective, learn more quickly, understand a new technology better, and discover and remove common problems or impediments across the teams. The facilitating team can also help to discover gaps or inconsistencies in existing components and services used by other teams.

Teams that interact using the facilitating mode typically work across many other teams, detecting and reducing cross-team problems and helping to inform the direction and capabilities of things like code libraries, APIs, and platforms provided as a service by other teams or organizations.

> Facilitating: helping (or being helped by) another team to clear impediments

A team with a facilitating remit does not take part in building the main software systems, supporting components, or platform but, instead, focuses on the quality of interactions between other teams building and running the software. For example, a team facilitating the effectiveness of three stream-aligned teams (see Chapter 5) might find that the logging service provided by the platform is quite difficult to configure: all three teams find it difficult to use. The team helping the three teams can then facilitate some improvements to the logging service from the platform.

Because only one of the two teams in a facilitation team interaction is building the main software systems, the effects of Conway's law have already been anticipated: the team doing the facilitating helps to define and clarify the communication between other teams based on the system desired architecture.

Table7.3: Advantages and Disadvantages of Facilitation Mode

Advantages	Disadvantages
• Unblocking of stream-aligned teams to increase flow • Detection of gaps and misaligned capabilities or features in components and platforms	• Requires experienced staff to not work on "building" or "running" things • The interaction may be unfamiliar or strange to one or both teams involved in facilitation
Constraint: A team should expect to use the facilitating interaction mode with a small number of other teams simultaneously, whether consuming or providing the facilitation.	
Typical Uses: An enabling team helping a stream-aligned, complicated-subsystem, or platform team; or a stream-aligned, complicated-subsystem, or platform team helping a stream-aligned team.	

Team Behaviors for Each Interaction Mode

Each team-interaction mode works best with a corresponding set of team behaviors. These team behaviors can be thought of as "styles" of behavior, rather like a concert band adopting different styles of musical performance to suit the context: jazz, swing, orchestral film score, and so on. The band (or team) is made up of the same people, but the style they adopt as a group changes depending on the kind of effect they need to have. This also holds for situations where the band (team) needs to perform together with another group, such as a quartet or choir: the performance style of the band changes to enable the two combined groups to succeed in their performance.

Just as a concert band changes its performance style to suit the needs of the music it is playing and the other groups it is performing with, a team following the Team Topologies approach to software delivery should adopt different "styles" of team behavior depending on which other team or teams it is interacting with.

Leading technologist James Urquhart, writing about team intercommunication with Conway's law in mind, describes the need for "a communication backchannel that avoids much of the politics, bandwidth constraints, and simple inefficiency of human-to-human communication."[4] This is exactly the kind of outcome this chapter's well-defined team interactions should provide. Furthermore, behavioral studies suggest that humans work best with others when we can predict their behavior. As humans, we can build trust by providing consistent experiences for others in the organization. Clear roles and responsibility boundaries help this by defining expected behavior and avoiding what some refer to as "invisible electric fences."[5]

> **TIP**
>
> **Promise theory as a way to design systems for team interaction.**
> Promise theory—devised by technologist and researcher Mark Burgess—explains how and why it is preferable to construct inter-team relationships in terms of promises rather than in terms of commands and enforceable contracts. For example, by adhering to the meaning of the major/minor/patch/build numbering indicated by semantic versioning (SemVer), the team promises not to break software that depends on their code.[6]

Team Behaviors for Collaboration Mode: "High Interaction and Mutual Respect"

Teams interacting using the collaboration mode should expect to have high interaction and mutual respect with the collaborating team. This typically means that team members should expect activities to take much longer than they might expect as the "boundary spanning" aspects of collaboration discover and solve previously unknown problems. Rewarding one team for the work of the other team can help to align behaviors—what Don Reinertsen, author of *Principles of Product Development Flow*, calls the "Principle of Overlapping Measurement."[7]

> **TIP**
>
> **How to train for collaboration mode.**
> Some training or coaching in basic collaboration skills such as pair programming, mob programming, and whiteboard sketching—together with specific training around boundary-spanning collaboration—can be valuable for teams interacting using collaboration mode.

Team Behaviors for X-as-a-Service Mode: "Emphasize the User Experience"

Teams interacting using the X-as-a-Service mode should expect to emphasize the user experience of the thing being provided as a service. For example, if a platform team is providing a set of dynamic cloud testing environments for a stream-aligned team to use, both the platform team and the stream-aligned team should emphasize the experience of interacting with the environments: what the API feels like, how easy it is to see the resources being used, how compelling the features are to use, etc. Clearly, the functionality of the platform is also important, but in order to drive the best and most fruitful interaction between teams, a focus on the experience of using the platform is essential.

> **TIP**
>
> **How to train for X-as-a-Service mode.**
> Some training or coaching in core user-experience (UX) and developer-experience (DevEx) practices can be valuable for teams interacting using X-as-a-Service mode.

Team Behaviors for Facilitating Mode: "Help and Be Helped"

Teams interacting using the facilitating mode should expect to help and be helped. Let's say that a stream-aligned team is being helped by an enabling team to adopt new practices. People in the stream-aligned team need to be open to being helped by the enabling team; they need to have an open mind to new approaches and be aware that the enabling team has probably seen some better approaches.

Choosing Suitable Team Interaction Modes

Each of the four fundamental team topologies—stream aligned, enabling, complicated subsystem, and platform—have certain characteristic behaviors that make them work well in an organizational context. Sometimes, a team may need to adopt a different mode of interaction with other teams (either temporarily or on a permanent basis) in order to improve outcomes.

Each fundamental team topology is likely to encounter different interaction modes. Aligning team interactions to these three modes helps ensure that the teams are operating as effectively as possible for their current organizational purpose. Figure 7.5 (see page 145) shows the primary interaction modes for each of the four fundamental team topologies.

The typical and occasional team interaction modes of the fundamental team topologies can be mapped to the essential team interaction modes as shown in Table 7.4.

Table 7.4: Team interaction modes of the fundamental team topologies

	Collaboration	X-as-a-Service	Facilitating
Stream-aligned	Typical	Typical	Occasional
Enabling	Occasional		Typical
Complicated-subsystem	Occasional	Typical	
Platform	Occasional	Typical	

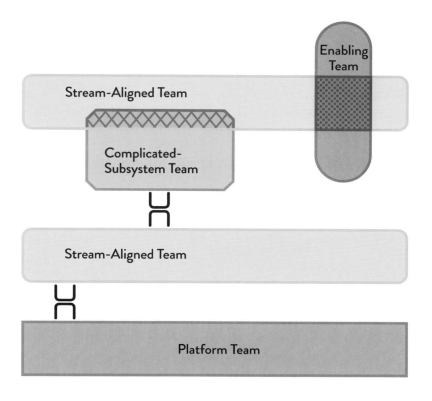

**Figure 7.5: Primary Interaction Modes for the
Four Fundamental Team Topologies**

Stream-aligned teams use X-as-a-Service or collaboration; enabling teams
use facilitation; complicated-subsystem teams use X-as-a-Service; platform
teams use X-as-a-Service for teams that consume the platform.

Table 7.4 provides a useful reminder of how different teams can expect to interact with other teams in the organization. For example, a stream-aligned team can typically expect to interact with other teams using either collaboration or X-as-a-Service, whereas a platform team mostly expects to interact using X-as-a-Service. This gives some further hints for the kinds of interpersonal skills likely to be needed for each type of team: platform teams will need strong product- and service-management expertise, whereas enabling teams will need people with strong mentoring and facilitating experience.

Choosing Basic Team Organization

With an understanding of the team interaction modes, we can choose an initial organization design that is likely to help produce the software architecture required. Expectations should be set with coworkers that the interaction modes and team structures will need to change at least a little as the organization "senses" whether the boundaries chosen are in fact the best boundaries.

CASE STUDY: TEAM INTERACTION DIVERSITY AT IBM AROUND 2014

Eric Minick, Program Director for Continuous Delivery, IBM

Since 2013, Eric Minick has led the introduction and dissemination of new practices across the worldwide IBM technical teams.

When I joined IBM in 2013, the enterprise software industry was going through some significant changes brought about by cloud technologies and ubiquitous automation. Part of my role at the time was to help bring then-new DevOps and Agile practices to 40,000 developers in several dozen locations (on six continents). There were many different kinds of team interactions happening, and so, to help encourage a shift to the newer ways of working, we had an "advocates" team (see Figure 7.6).

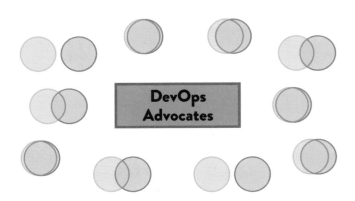

Figure 7.6: Team Interaction Modes at IBM around 2014
Team interaction modes at IBM around 2014, with a team of "DevOps advocates" coordinating and facilitating learning and team changes.

The advocates team included a handful of full-time people and some part-timers. It gathered successful patterns from various teams around the world to encourage and educate others, helping the ideas to diffuse through the organization at IBM. Its approach included formal training for teams and their executives. Meanwhile, there was a drumbeat of content like internal webinars that would draw an audience of thousands of technologists.

The advocates team probably doesn't fit neatly as a team topology because we saw ourselves as a temporary team that should not be needed in a few years' time, or as I said on Twitter at the time: The goal for a "DevOps Team" should be to put itself out of business by enabling the rest of the org.

Use the Reverse Conway Maneuver with Collaboration and Facilitating Interactions

When we undertake a reverse Conway maneuver (see Chapter 2), the homomorphic pull of self-similarity that Conway's law identifies is anticipated: the organization is set up to match the communication paths needed in the software and systems architecture. However, a new architecture cannot be expected to emerge as soon as a new team structure has been devised and implemented. Precisely due to the forces behind Conway's law, the existing software architecture will initially "push back" against the new team structures.

To help make the new organizational structure work—and to sense whether the new responsibility boundaries are actually correct—the reverse Conway maneuver should be used with temporary but explicit collaboration modes between the teams building the software, along with one or more enabling teams (and possibly other teams) acting in a facilitating mode. By using temporary, explicit collaboration across the new boundaries and by using a high degree of facilitating for the stream-aligned and complicated-subsystem teams, any problems with the new responsibility boundaries can be quickly identified, giving the team the opportunity to adjust the design earlier, before too much has been built.

The team responsibilities for software subsystems during the collaboration phase may need to be back to front to begin with so that the team ownership can be effective long term. For example, let's say that a large software monolith needs to be split into separate segments (aligned to streams, components, or new aspects of a platform). Teams that "logically" own a higher-level component may need to work on the lower layer (platform) for a period of time in order to split out that code, especially if they wrote the too-coupled code in the first place. As the collaboration period progresses, the team that logically owns the lower layer can take on more responsibility from the original team until the new team takes full ownership of the lower layer.

Discover Effective APIs between Teams by Deliberate Evolution of Team Topologies

As we saw in Chapter 5, a dedicated architecture team is usually an anti-pattern to be avoided. However, a small group of software and systems architects can be hugely effective within an organization when the remit of architecture is to discover, adjust, and reshape the interactions between teams, and therefore, the architecture of the system.

This is because with Conway's law in force within a system-building organization, the architecture of the organization is the architecture of the system. Or, as Ruth Malan puts it, "[t]he organizational divides are going to drive the true seams in the system."[8] Allan Kelly—longtime advocate of using the reverse Conway manuever to shape teams, says: "someone who claims to be an Architect needs both technical and social skills . . . . They also need a remit that is broader than pure technology—they need to have a say in business strategies, organizational structures, and personnel issues, i.e., they need to be a manager too."[9]

The architect should be thinking: "Which team interaction modes are appropriate for these two teams? What kind of communication do we need between these two parts of the system, between these two teams?" The architect in an organization following the Team Topologies approach is therefore the designer of team APIs that anticipate the intended software architecture.

Effectively, instead of trying to rely entirely on individuals within teams to perform boundary spanning (which can be stressful and needs both good social and technical skills), use people skilled in API design to design the APIs between teams within the organization.

Choose Team Interaction Modes to Reduce Uncertainty and Enhance Flow

The different team interaction modes have different characteristics, making them suitable for different kinds of activities or goals. In this section, we identify which team interactions modes to use in different circumstances.

Use the Collaboration Mode to Discover Viable X-as-a-Service Interactions

The X-as-a-Service interaction mode can be highly effective in helping software-delivery teams achieve fast flow. However, as with any service, if the service boundaries are not well drawn and the service attempts to provide either too much or too little without enough flexibility, the X-as-a-Service interaction will not be effective; the service will not meet the needs of consuming teams.

To address the problem of poorly drawn service boundaries, the collaboration team interaction mode can be used to help redraw service boundaries in a new place, either contracting or expanding the remit of the service (or adding more flexibility) in order to make the service more suitable for consuming teams. In fact, ongoing, lightweight collaboration interactions at service boundaries should be expected to make sure that all services are as effective as they can be. We want "just enough" collaboration at the service boundaries to adjust the scope of the service to meet the needs of consuming and providing teams.

If an organization is trying to establish a new X-as-a-Service interaction, the same pattern applies: collaborate closely to establish viable "as a service" boundaries and then continue with lightweight collaboration to validate that the boundaries are effective.

The collaboration team interaction mode can be used to drive the rate of innovation of both application and platform/infrastructure, which is particularly useful for new and emerging products or service offerings.

> **TIP**
>
> Collaborate on potentially ambiguous interfaces until the interfaces are proven stable and functional.

Change the Team Interaction Mode Temporarily to Help a Team Grow Experience and Empathy

If the current mode of interaction between teams has been in place for some time and possibly needs some revitalization, changing the interaction mode temporarily can help team members refresh and grow their experience, and increase empathy for the other team. Evan Wiley of Pivotal describes how, for a team with a dependency on another team, "those teams may arrange to swap pairs, and somebody might go from one team to another team for a few days or a week to get the feature done."[10] As Heidi Helfand puts it, "when you deliberately plan out the [team changes] in your organization, you provide new learning opportunities for people."[11]

It is vitally important that the changes are deliberate (and probably also temporary) with the full consent, understanding, and enthusiasm of the people involved. *Dynamic Reteaming* by Heidi Helfand provides many useful recommendations for making team changes as smooth as possible.

Use Awkwardness in Team Interactions to Sense Missing Capabilities and Misplaced Boundaries

The patterns of team interactions can be used to detect and respond to problems with the design of the system, potentially anticipating software problems before the code reaches production.

Let's consider two examples:

1. A stream-aligned team that should be consuming a calculation component "as a service" from a complicated-subsystem team is spending significant amounts of time on instant messenger and in person talking to the complicated-subsystem team to try to use the component.
2. A platform team expects to be collaborating closely with a stream-aligned team in order to assess a new technology approach but is getting little interaction from the other team.

In the first case, we know that the X-as-a-Service interaction should be low friction and should need only occasional or limited communication. If the stream-aligned team is spending many hours trying to use a component, this is a signal that something is amiss: Is the component boundary in the right place? Is the component API well specified? Is the component easy enough to use? Does the complicated-subsystem team have a missing capability within the team, such as UX or DevEx?

In the second example, the platform team is expecting significant communication with the stream-aligned team, because they are supposed to be using the collaboration interaction mode to discover new technology solutions together. In this case, the absence of inter-team communication is a sign that something is wrong in the stream-aligned team: Do they understand the value of adopting the collaboration mode at this point? Do they have enough skills to undertake this collaboration, or is another team better suited? Is the boundary that the teams are trying to bridge too ambitious?

As Don Reinertsen says, "We need to be alert for the white space between the roles, gaps that nobody feels responsible for."[12]

> **TIP**
>
> Techniques from domain-driven design (DDD) such as event storming and context mapping can help accelerate awareness of appropriate boundaries. See Chapter 6 for more details on DDD.

Summary: Three Well-Defined Team Interaction Modes

An effective, modern organization building and running software is a product of the interactions between teams. Yet many organizations fail to define what good team interactions look like, resulting in confusion, annoyance, and ineffectiveness. Simply defining a set of teams with responsibility boundaries is not enough to produce an effective sociotechnical system; it is also necessary to define sensible and effective interactions between teams.

In this chapter, we've seen how three core team interaction modes provide the clarity needed for all team interactions within the organization:

- **Collaboration:** two teams work closely together for a defined period to discover new patterns, approaches, and limitations. Responsibility is shared and boundaries blurred, but problems are solved rapidly and the organization learns quickly.
- **X-as-a-Service:** one team consumes something (such as a service or an API) provided "as a service" from another team. Responsibilities are clearly delineated and—if the boundary is effective—the consuming team can deliver rapidly. The team providing the service seeks to make their service as easy to consume as possible.
- **Facilitating:** one team helps another team to learn or adopt new approaches for a defined period of time. The team providing the facilitation aims to make the other team self-sufficient as soon as possible, while the team receiving the facilitation has an open-minded attitude to learning.

The combination of well-defined team types and well-defined team interactions provides a clear and powerful way to promote team-based organizational effectiveness, avoiding the ambiguities and conflicts that many organizations experience.

8

Evolve Team Structures with Organizational Sensing

The design...is almost never the best possible, [so] the prevailing system concept may need to change. Therefore, flexibility of organization is important to effective design.

—**Mel Conway**, "How Do Committees Invent?"

Modern organizations face huge challenges in responding to rapid changes in regulatory and market conditions, customer and user demands, rapidly-moving trends, and powerful shifts in technology capabilities. A successful modern organization needs to be able to shape-shift to deal with these changing circumstances by designing for adaptability. Therefore, when designing modern organizations for building and running software systems, the most important thing is not the shape of the organization itself but the decision rules and heuristics used to adapt and change the organization as new challenges arise; that is, we need to design the design rules, not just the organization.

This chapter covers a set of design rules for modern, software-powered organizations, taking into account the true implications of Conway's law, team-first decision-making, and the four fundamental team topologies described in Chapter 5.

How Much Collaboration Is Right for Each Team Interaction?

As we saw in Chapter 7, the two primary interaction modes for teams are collaboration, where two teams with different skills come together to work on something, and X-as-a-Service, where one team provides and one team consumes, and there doesn't need to be very much collaboration at all. It's important to recognize that neither mode is better or worse than the other; they simply are useful for different kinds of work.

Collaboration is good for rapid discovery and avoiding hand-offs and delays, but the downside is a higher level of cognitive load. Each side of the collaboration needs to understand more about the other side, so the team members have to retain more in their heads. However, this "collaboration tax" is worth it if the organization wants to innovate very rapidly.

By contrast, with X-as-a-Service there is great clarity about which team owns what. There is also less mental context needed for each team, so the cognitive load on each side of the relationship is lower. It's likely that as a whole, the teams innovate more slowly with X-as-a-Service than collaboration, precisely because their interaction is mediated and defined by a clean API that has locked down the interaction possibilities. X-as-a-Service is best for situations where predictable delivery is more important than rapid discovery.

This approach is backed by recent research into high-performing organizations presented in *Accelerate*:

> In teams which score highly on architectural capabilities [which directly lead to higher performance], little communication is required between delivery teams to get their work done, and the architecture of the system is designed to enable teams to test, deploy, and change their systems without dependencies on other teams. In other words, architecture and teams are loosely coupled."[1]

TIP

Restrict any ongoing collaboration between teams to explicit valuable activity.

Collaboration is expensive. Unnecessary collaboration is particularly expensive, especially as it can mask or hide deficiencies in underlying platforms or capabilities. Any ongoing collaboration activity must, therefore, be justified as valuable discovery, valuable capability building, or valuable deficiency-filling activity.

To reach the level of a high-performing organization, it is important to decide how much collaboration is appropriate for each team-to-team interaction. Should Team A simply be able to consume services from Team B with little effort? If they should but cannot yet, should Team A collaborate with Team B for a short time (Three weeks? Three months?) in order to better define the API for Team B and enable Team A to consume it "as a service"? Exactly what should the teams collaborate on, bearing in mind that the collaboration will likely tend to blur the boundaries of each part of the system between Team A and Team B?

CASE STUDY: ADOPTION OF KUBERNETES TO DRIVE ORGANIZATIONAL CHANGE AT USWITCH

Paul Ingles, Head of Engineering, uSwitch

Paul Ingles, at consumer-rating service uSwitch, describes how, after many years of slowly increasing complexity, they realized that Dev teams were having to understand too much of the underlying technology stack to be properly effective.

What was needed was a platform abstraction that minimized Dev team cognitive load.[2] They adopted a new cloud infrastructure abstraction (called Kubernetes) in order to help with this shift: "We didn't change our organization because we wanted to use Kubernetes; we used Kubernetes because we wanted to change our organization."[3]

This deliberate use of a change in team interaction to force a beneficial change in delivery capability is the essence of strong, strategic technology leadership.

Accelerate Learning and Adoption of New Practices

Deliberately changing the interaction mode of two teams to collaboration can be a powerful organizational enabler for rapid learning and adoption of new practices and approaches. If one team has significant experience in a valuable set of practices—such as test automation—from which the second team would benefit, then bringing the two teams together in collaboration mode for a few months can not only help to improve and define the API between the teams but also produce a step change in the capability of the second team.

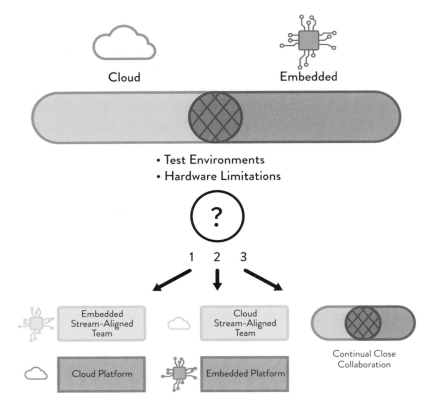

Figure 8.1: Collaboration between Cloud and Embedded Teams

Two teams ("cloud" and "embedded") collaborate to share practices and increase awareness. The results will include heightened awareness of the options for future team interactions: (1) treat the cloud software as a platform for the embedded team to use, (2) treat the embedded devices as a platform for the cloud team to use, or (3) continue with close collaboration.

This "deliberate collaboration" is particularly useful where two groups have very different prior experience due to the prevailing practices around their respective technologies.

Consider (as shown in Figure 8.1) a team that is adept at building cloud-based software and is building some cloud-hosted metric collection and analytics software that receives data from a fleet of IoT devices running embedded software. Bringing this team together to collaborate closely with a team of embedded software specialists—whose experience is much more low level—would not only help both teams to better understand the challenges across this embedded/cloud technology divide but also bring benefits around test automation.

The cloud team probably treats test environments as ephemeral and dynamic, and can help the embedded team take a more nimble approach to testing. In return, the embedded team can help the cloud team understand the memory and processing restrictions of the embedded IoT devices and tailor their code and protocols to better suit the limited hardware.

This collaboration period will also help the organization assess whether the cloud software or the embedded devices can and should be treated as a platform (in the sense used in this book) with the corresponding behaviors from the platform-providing team. The alternative is, of course, for the teams to continue to collaborate, possibly with an enabling team providing some mediation. As the collaboration continues, the teams may realize that their respective change cadences are increasingly aligning, in which case they may decide to form a "paired" set of teams, both stream aligned.

CASE STUDY: EVOLUTION OF TEAM TOPOLOGIES AT TRANSUNION (PART 2)

Dave Hotchkiss, Platform Build Manager, TransUnion

(Continued from Chapter 4)

At the start of our transformation in 2014, we realized that the development (Dev) and operations (Ops) groups were separated by a large gap. We knew that a separate team of evangelists could help bring Dev and Ops closer together; but in our case, we decided to use two teams, because the gap was so wide.

From the Dev group we created a system-build (SB) team, and from the Ops group we created a platform-build (PB) team. We then focused on getting SB and PB collaborating closely, which was a simpler problem to solve initially than getting all the Dev and Ops teams to collaborate (see Figure 8.2 on page 158).

We drew out a timeline of the team evolution, inspired by the DevOps Team Topologies patterns. We expected to need to focus on awareness or operability within Dev teams to begin with, so our initial team evolution had the SB team collaborating closely with the Dev teams and the PB team. This really helped improve things, like deployment automation, metrics, logging, and other operational aspects (see Figure 8.3 on page 158).

Expected Evolution (2014)

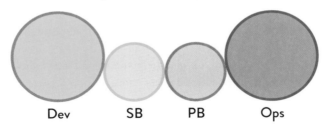

Dev   SB   PB   Ops

Figure 8.2: System-Build and Platform-Build Team at TransUnion
A team from Dev (SB) and a team from Ops (PB) exploring close interactions.

Expected in 6+ months; Actual realization 2 years

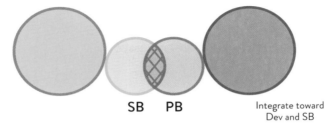

SB   PB   Integrate toward
                                     Dev and SB

**Figure 8.3: System-Build and Platform-Build Team
Collaboration at TransUnion**
The two teams, SB and PB, collaborating closely.

Expected in 12+ months; Actual realization 4 years

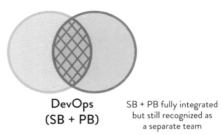

DevOps   SB + PB fully integrated
(SB + PB)   but still recognized as
                     a separate team

Figure 8.4: System-Build and Platform-Build Teams Merged at TransUnion
The SB and PB teams merged, helping to bring Dev and Ops together.

Back in 2014, we expected to have evolved the SB and PB teams to a nice enabling team within twelve months. As it happened, this transition took quite a bit longer than we initially thought (three years longer!) as we started to move our services to Azure; but by early 2018, we had made this work (see Figure 8.4 on page 158). The benefits to the business were really clear: safer, more regular production changes, fewer deployment mistakes, and better traceability of changes (essential in the highly regulated financial sector in which TransUnion operates).

By late 2018, we had gone even further, finally merging the SB team back into the Dev teams and PB into the Ops teams, bringing higher levels of operational awareness and accountability, and leaving Ops to manage the underlying platform, with some strategic infrastructure running in Azure Cloud (see Figure 8.5).

2018

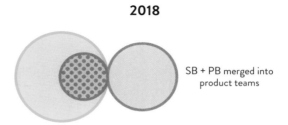

SB + PB merged into
product teams

Figure 8.5: System-Build and Platform-Build Teams Merged Back into Dev and Ops at TransUnion
The SB and PB teams merged back into Dev and Ops, providing Platform-as-a-Service.

Our early realization that this should be an evolution of teams was really important for our success. People knew that things would take some time, and the clear but changing responsibility boundaries helped people to understand their part in the process.

Constant Evolution of Team Topologies

Collaboration is costly but good for discovery of new approaches, and X-as-a-Service is good for predictable delivery; so teams can be set up to match the needs of each area of the software system and each team. But what happens when the requirements or operating context changes?

Figure 8.6: Evolution of Team Topologies

The evolution of Team Topologies from close collaboration to limited collaboration (discovery) through to X-as-a-Service for established, predictable delivery.

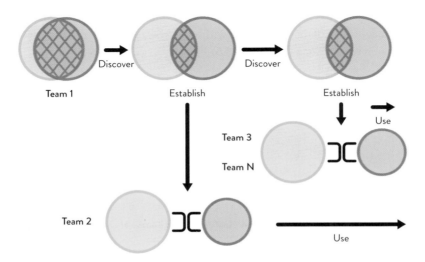

Figure 8.7: Evolution of Team Topologies in an Enterprise

Team 1 continues to collaborate with a platform team, discovering new patterns and ways of using new technologies. This discovery activity eventually enables Team 2 to adopt an X-as-a-Service relationship with the platform team. Later, Teams 3 and beyond adopt a later version of the platform, using it as a service without having to collaborate closely with the platform team.

Interaction modes of different teams should be expected to change regularly, depending on what the teams need to achieve. If a team needs to explore part of the technology stack or part of the logical domain model currently handled by another team, then they should agree to use collaboration mode for a specific period of time. If a team needs to increase its delivery predictability following successful discovery of new approaches with another team, then it should move away from collaboration mode toward X-as-a-Service to help define the API between the teams.

In this way, teams should expect to adopt different interaction modes for periods of time depending on what they need to achieve. Of course, Conway's law tells us that during the discovery and rapid learning taking place as part of collaboration mode, the responsibilities and architecture of the software is likely to be more "blended together" compared to when the teams are interacting using X-as-a-Service. By anticipating this fuzziness, some awkward team interactions ("the API is not well designed" and so forth) can be avoided by tightening up the API as the team moves to X-as-a-Service.

The evolution of team topologies from close collaboration to limited collaboration to X-as-a-Service can be visualized in Figure 8.6 (see page 160).

Initial close collaboration evolves into more limited collaboration on a smaller number of things as the technology and product is better understood through discovery, and it further evolves into X-as-a-Service once the product or service boundary is more established.

In a larger enterprise, this "discover to establish" pattern is expected to happen all the time with different teams at different stages of development. There should be multiple discovery activities happening simultaneously, with other teams taking advantage of well-defined APIs to be able to consume things as a service, as shown in Figure 8.7 (see page 160).

In some organizations, teams may operate on a permanent basis with many teams using collaboration, especially if the rate of innovation is very high. Other organizations may have a tendency toward mostly X-as-a-Service interactions, because they have a well-defined problem space and mostly need to execute on well-understood business problems. The key point here is that teams need different interaction modes depending on what they need to achieve.

Ultimately, by expecting and encouraging team interactions to move between collaboration and X-as-a-Service for specific reasons, organizations can achieve agility.

Keeping the interrelations between teams in the organization well defined and dynamic provides the foundation for what Jeff Sussna calls a "continuous design capability" for external and internal contexts.[4] This dynamic reshaping provides a key strategic capability. John Kotter, expert in organizational change, says: "I think of [strategy] as an ongoing process of 'searching, doing, learning, and modifying' . . . . The more the organization exercises its strategy skills, the more adept it becomes at dealing with a hypercompetitive environment."[5]

> **_TIP_**
>
> Evolve different team topologies for different parts of the organization at different times to match the team purpose and context.

We have seen that team interactions should explicitly evolve over time, depending on what the teams are doing. In a discovery phase, some degree of collaboration is expected, but close collaboration often doesn't scale across the organization. The aim should be to try to establish a well-defined and capable platform that many teams can simply use as a service.

Organizations should aim to move from discovery activities to establish predictable delivery over time as new commodity services and platforms become available. The implication for organizations is that the experience of people in different teams within the organization will differ depending on the kind of thing they're working on at that point in time. Not all teams will interact with other teams in the same way, and that is what we want.

Different topologies and different team interactions for different parts of an organization need to evolve at different times based on what they are doing and what they are trying to achieve. The organization must ask itself: "Are we trying to discover things? And how rapidly do we need to discover them?" There might be times when there is a need to colocate people—at the same desks or simply on the same floor in the same building—to produce the kind of proximity that encourages the right amount of collaboration. At other times, teams might move to separate floors or even separate buildings in order to help enforce an API boundary; a slight distance in terms of communication can help do that (see Chapter 3 for more details on office layouts).

The team topologies within an organization change slowly over several months, not every day or every week. Over a few months, change should be encouraged in the team interaction modes, and a corresponding change should be expected in the software architecture.

CASE STUDY: SKY BETTING & GAMING—PLATFORM FEATURE TEAMS (PART 2)

Michael Maibaum, Chief Architect, Sky Betting & Gaming

(Continued from Chapter 5)

Platform Evolution had reached a tipping point, and we had a choice to make: we could dissolve the team and make each of the now relatively large product teams responsible for their own configuration management, or we could try and figure out how to support those teams more effectively—to enable them to accelerate delivery with high quality and reliability.

We decided that the Platform Evolution team had to change, becoming a product team with services and support capabilities, in order to think and design the things they were working on as services to be consumed by other teams. In short, the team had to focus on features that drive value to the business.

Platform Evolution became Platform Services and began to work with a very different worldview. Their mission was to provide services designed to support other teams with features and capabilities driven by their customers. In other words, Platform Services became a product-driven team.

Alongside the work to break down our Chef monolith, Platform Services developed a number of customer-focused services, providing centralized value-add services to teams, including AWS integrations, build and test environments, logging platforms, and much more. In each case, Platform Services took a fundamental capability that teams needed (and could, in theory, build for themselves) and provided a managed service equivalent. Platform Services took the time to provide bespoke adaptations that delivery teams needed to make the standard tool more valuable and easier to use in the SB&G environment; and in doing so, saved the business the overhead of repeating those solutions in many teams around the business.

Through this period, Platform Evolution/Services were most closely aligned with the in-house software teams. It was often a point of debate and contention on the appropriate boundaries of responsibility, particularly between our infrastructure team and Platform Services. Platform Services was building things like firewall and load-balancer automation, tools to support our increasing usage of AWS, secrets management and PKI, but it was often struggling with the organizational boundaries between it and the infrastructure team. The question arose of how much should infrastructure be responsible for in the "platform layer"? And—slightly more delicately—were they organized in a way to support products?

Once this conversation started, it became clear that it overlapped with conversations within our infrastructure team about how they should be organized. Infrastructure was the last significant function in the business with a clear delivery/operations split in the team, and there was an appetite to try something different. Infrastructure reorganized around products and services; smaller teams owned the end-to-end life cycle of a coherent set of related things, with a drive to make them better for their customers around the business. As part of that transformation, it also became obvious where Platform Services fit best—not as one team between infrastructure and the rest of technology but as part of the infrastructure function.

Some services—like load balancer and firewall automation—found a more natural home in one of our networking-related squads, while some remained in the two Platform Services squads: Platform Engineering and Delivery Engineering. We seeded automation engineers into infrastructure squads around services that had never had that capability, and developed an infrastructure product function to support the team's engagement with the wider business.

We now have infrastructure-platform feature teams, just like we have customer-facing product feature teams; and while the change hasn't been simple or without its challenges, it's clear from the level of engagement, sense of ownership, and reduced friction with other areas of the business that the change has been transformative. From the other areas of the business, it's now clear who to talk to and what that team is doing and why, when it often wasn't before, because it was all just "infrastructure."

Combining Team Topologies for Greater Effectiveness

At any one time, different teams within an organization will have different interaction and collaboration needs. Different kinds of team topologies should be expected to be seen simultaneously. Some degree of collaboration between teams is expected, but collaboration often doesn't scale across the organization; and consuming things as a service is often more effective as the number of teams increases.

For example, perhaps we have four stream-aligned teams building different parts of the software system. One of the teams may be in collaboration mode with the platform team, undertaking some discovery work on new logging technology, while the other three teams are simply consuming the platform in X-as-a-Service mode.

Superimposed on the same diagram, the interactions might look like this: The first stream-aligned team has a collaboration interaction with the platform team—the teams collaborate on new technology approaches and learn new techniques rapidly. The stream-aligned team is supported by a enabling team. The other three stream-aligned teams treat the platform as a service and are also supported by the enabling team. These different interactions are present to reflect the nature of the work being undertaken by the stream-aligned teams and the kind of interactions present in the software they are building.

In this example, there are three different kinds of team interactions happening simultaneously: the stream-aligned teams are experiencing a facilitating interaction with the enabling team, and three of the four stream-aligned teams expect an X-as-a-Service interaction with the platform, leaving one stream-aligned team to undertake the discovery work with the platform team via a collaboration interaction.

Because the interaction modes are clear and explicit, and because these are mapped to well-defined purposes, people on different teams within the organization understand why they interact in different ways with other teams. This helps to increase engagement within teams and to enable teams to use any friction from the interactions as signals to detect a range of problems. We explore some of these signals in the next section.

Triggers for Evolution of Team Topologies

Using the advice from Chapter 5, it is fairly straightforward to map an organization's structure to the four fundamental team topologies at a specific point in time, but it's often difficult to have the required organizational self-awareness to detect when it's time to evolve the team structure. There are some situations that act as triggers to redesign team topologies within the organization. Learning to recognize these will help an organization continue to adapt and evolve with its needs.

Trigger: Software Has Grown Too Large for One Team

Symptoms
- A startup company grows beyond fifteen people (Dunbar's number).

- Other teams spend lots of time waiting on a single team to undertake changes.
- Changes to certain components or workflows in the system routinely get assigned to the same people, even when they're already busy or away.
- Team members complain about lack of system documentation.

Context

Successful software products tend to grow larger and larger as more features get added and more customers adopt the product. While initially it is possible that everyone in the product team has a fairly broad understanding of the codebase, that becomes increasingly more difficult over time.

This can lead to an (often unspoken) specialization within the team regarding different components of the system. Requests that require changes to a specific component or workflow routinely get assigned to the same team member(s), because they will be able to deliver faster than other team members.

This reinforcing cycle of specialization is a local optimization ("get this request delivered quickly") that can negatively affect the team's overall flow of work when planning gets dictated by "who knows what" rather than "what's the highest priority work we need to do now." This level of specialization introduces bottlenecks in delivery (as storied in *The Phoenix Project* and explained in *The DevOps Handbook*). The routine aspect can also negatively affect individual motivation.

Another aspect at play occurs when the team no longer holds a holistic view of the system; thus, it loses the self-awareness to realize when the system has become too large. While there is some correlation between system size in terms of lines of code or features, it is the limit on cognitive capacity to handle changes to the system in an effective way that is most of concern here.

Trigger: Delivery Cadence Is Becoming Slower

Symptoms

- Team members qualitatively feel it takes longer to release changes than it used to.
- Team velocity or throughput metrics show a clear downward variation compared to one year ago. (There is always some variation, so make sure it's not accidental.)

- Team members complain that the delivery process used to be simpler, with fewer steps.
- Work in progress keeps increasing, with many changes waiting for another team's action.

Context

A long-lived, high-performing product team should be able to steadily improve their delivery cadence as they find ways to work more efficiently together and remove bottlenecks in delivery. However, a pre-requisite for these teams to flourish is to grant them autonomy over the entire life cycle of the product. This means no hard dependencies on external teams, such as waiting for another team to create new infrastructure. Being able to self-serve new infrastructure via an internal platform is a soft dependency (assuming the provisioning self-service is maintained by a platform team).

This level of autonomy is difficult to achieve in many organizations. In fact, it's common to see the opposite: reducing autonomy by introducing new hard dependencies between teams. It could be an attempt at increasing test coverage by creating a quality assurance (QA) team to centralize testing of all the products and, theoretically, allocate work to testers more efficiently. While such a goal is laudable, this team design introduces a "functional silo" (QA), whereby all teams delivering software will need to wait on the QA team to be available to test their updates.

The emergence of DevOps highlighted the divide between development and operations teams in the 2010s, but it's the same problem—to a greater or lesser extent—for all other silos that intervene in the product delivery life cycle.

Note that it's also possible that delivery has slowed down because of accrued technical debt. In this scenario, the complexity of the codebase might reach a state where even small changes are costly and frequently cause regressions. That means deliveries take much longer to develop and stabilize than when the codebase was initially created.

Trigger: Multiple Business Services Rely On a Large Set of Underlying Services

Symptoms
- Stream-aligned teams have limited visibility of end-to-end flow within their service area.

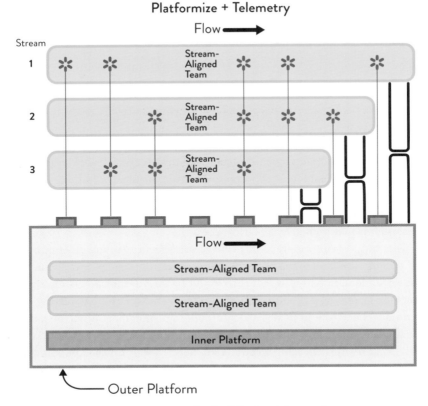

Figure 8.8: Example of a "Platform Wrapper"

Increase flow predictability in higher-level business services (streams) through
the use of a "platform wrapper" to "platformize" the lower-level services and APIs,
allowing the streams to treat all their dependencies as a single platform with a
holistic roadmap and consistent DevEx. The streams also have rich telemetry
to track flow and resource usage of the platform.

- It becomes difficult to achieve a smooth and rapid flow of change due
  to the number and complexity of subsystem integrations.
- Attempts to "reuse" an existing set of services and subsystems becomes
  more and more challenging.

Context

In some highly regulated industry sectors, such as finance, insurance, legal, and
government, several different high-level business services may rely on a large set
of separate underlying services, APIs, or subsystems. For example, an insurance

company may need to conduct lengthy physical checks on factory machinery in order to provide an updated insurance quote; or a bank may need to await delivery of proof-of-address documents before opening a new bank account. The lower-level systems on which these higher-level business services rely might provide specialist payment mechanisms, data cleansing, identity verification, background legal checks, and so forth, each of which needs multiple teams working on it to evolve and sustain the service. Business process management (BPM)—perhaps augmented with machine learning (ML)—can help to automate some of the work in these cases; but engaged, aware teams still need to configure and test the BPM workflow scenarios. Some of these services and subsystems may be built and provided in house, but others may be provided by external suppliers.

In order to deliver useful business value, the higher-level streams need to integrate with many lower-level services (the realm of enterprise service management). If the streams have to integrate separately with each underlying service, it can be challenging to assess the effectiveness of flow and to diagnose errors in long-running processes that may have some human-decision input. For example, the underlying services may not expose tracking mechanisms or may each have a separate way to identify transactions.

The solution to these kinds of multi-service integration problems is twofold: (1) "Platformize" the lower-level services and APIs with a thin "platform wrapper" that provides a consistent developer experience (DevEx) for stream-aligned teams with things like request-tracking correlation IDs, health-check endpoints, test harnesses, service-level objectives, and diagnostic APIs. This "outer platform" is built on a still lower-level platform, but that remains hidden from stream-aligned teams. (2) Use stream-aligned teams for each high-level business service responsible for operational telemetry and fault diagnosis: building and evolving "just enough" telemetry integration and diagnostic capabilities to be able to detect where problems occur. Being in control of telemetry and diagnostics enables the stream-aligned teams to trace and improve the flow of change in their stream (see Figure 8.8 on page 168).

As part of the rich telemetry around each higher-level business service, the stream-aligned team builds and owns: (1) a lightweight digital-service "wrapper" that provides consistent logging time stamps, consistency in correlation IDs, request/response identification and logging, etc. when calling different underlying services and APIs in the platform; (2) logging, metrics, and dashboarding for the digital-service wrapper, allowing all "stream side" coordination to be tracked and traced (even if the "platform side" aspects are variable in their visibility initially).

To support a sustained and predictable flow in the higher-level business services, the platform wrapper must improve the DevEx around the platform services—consistency and standards around logging, metrics, dashboards, correlation IDs, etc.—so that greater traceability is possible from within the digital-service wrapper built by stream-aligned teams.

Self Steer Design and Development

Historically, many organizations have treated "develop" and "operate" as two distinct phases of software delivery, with very little interaction and certainly almost no feedback from operate to develop. Modern software delivery must take a completely different approach: the operation of the software should act as and provide valuable signals to the development activities. By treating operations as rich, sensory input to development, a cybernetic feedback system is set up that enables the organization to self steer.

Treat Teams and Team Interactions as Senses and Signals

With well-defined, stable teams taking effective ownership of different parts of the software systems and interacting using well-defined communication patterns, organizations can begin to activate a powerful strategic capability: organizational sensing.

Organizational sensing uses teams and their internal and external communication as the "senses" of the organization (sight, sound, touch, smell, taste)—what Peter Drucker calls "synthetic sense organs for the outside."[6] Without stable, well-defined neural communication pathways, no living organism can effectively sense anything. To sense things (and make sense of things), organisms need defined, reliable communication pathways. Similarly, with well-defined and stable communication pathways between teams, organizations can detect signals from across the organization and outside it, becoming something like an organism.

Many organizations—those with unstable and ill-defined teams, relying on key individuals and (often) suppressing the voices of large numbers of staff—are effectively "senseless" in both meanings of the word: they cannot sense their environmental situation, and what they do makes no sense. When speed of change was measured in months or years (as in the past), organizations could manage with very slow and limited environmental sensing; however, in today's network-connected world, high-fidelity sensing is crucial for organizational survival, just as an animal or other organism needs senses to survive in a competitive, dynamic natural environment.

Not only do organizations need to sense things with high fidelity, they also need to respond rapidly. Organisms generally have separate specialized organs for sensing (eyes, ears, etc.) and responding to input (limbs, body, etc.). The kinds of signals that different teams will be able to detect will differ depending on what the team does and how close it is to external customers, internal customers, other teams, and so on, but each team will be capable of providing sensory input to the organization and responding to the information by adjusting their team interaction patterns.

Thankfully, to help us with this task of what Naomi Stanford calls "environmental scanning,"[7] we have modern digital tools. Rich telemetry from digital metrics and logging helps teams achieve a real-time view of the health and performance of their software systems; and lightweight, network-connected devices (IoT and 4IR) provide regular sensor data from many thousands of physical locations.

So, what kinds of things should an organization sense? These questions can help an organization discover the answer:

- Have we misunderstood how users need/want to behave?
- Do we need to change team-interaction modes to enhance how the organization is working?
- Should we still be building thing X in house? Should we be renting it from an external provider?
- Is the close collaboration between Team A and Team B still effective? Should we move toward an X-as-a-Service model?
- Is the flow of work for Team C as smooth as it could be? What hampers flow?
- Does the platform for teams D, E, F, and G provide everything those teams need? Is an enabling team needed for a period of time?
- Are the promises between these two teams still valid and achievable? What needs to change to make the promises more realistic?

IT Operations as High-Value Sensory Input to Development

Moving quickly relies on sensory feedback about the environment. To sustain a fast flow of software changes, organizations must invest in organizational sensing and cybernetic control. A key aspect of this sensory feedback is the use of IT operations teams as high-fidelity sensory input for development teams, requiring joined-up communications between teams running systems (Ops) and teams building systems (Dev). Sadly, many organizations prevent themselves from moving quickly and safely. As Sriram Narayan says, "Project sponsors looking to reduce cost opt for a different team of lower-cost people for maintenance work. This is false economy. It hurts the larger business outcome and reduces IT agility."[8]

Instead of trying to optimize for lowest cost in so-called "maintenance" work, it is essential that organizations use signals from maintenance work as input to software-development activities. In the *The DevOps Handbook*, Gene Kim and colleagues define The Three Ways of DevOps for modern, high-performing organizations:[9]

1. **Systems thinking:** optimize for fast flow across the whole organization, not just in small parts
2. **Feedback loops:** Development informed and guided by Operations
3. **Culture of continual experimentation and learning:** sensing and feedback for every team interaction

The second and third ways rely on strong communication pathways between Ops and Dev. As we saw in Chapter 5, one of the simplest ways to ensure a continual flow of high-fidelity information from Ops to Dev is to have Ops and Dev on the same team, or at least aligned to the same stream of change as a stream-aligned pair of teams, with swarming for operational incidents. For organizations that have yet to move to this model or have a separate operations group, it is vital that communication paths are established and nurtured between Ops and Dev. This provides high-fidelity information about operational aspects, such as operability, reliability, usability, securability, and so forth, to enable Dev teams to course correct and navigate toward software designs that reduce operational overheads and improve reliability.

Treating Ops as an input to Dev requires a radical rethinking of the roles of these often-separate groups. Jeff Sussna, author of *Designing Delivery*, puts it like this: "Businesses normally treat operations as an output of design.... In order to empathize, though, one must be able to hear. In order to hear, one needs input from operations. Operations thus becomes an input to design."[10]

As Jeff implies, the aim here is to empathize with the various groups of users of the software and services we are building. By developing greater empa-

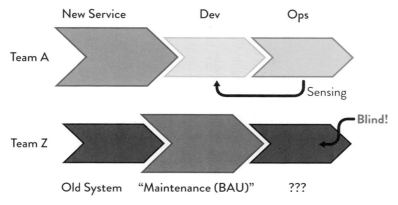

Figure 8.9: New-Service and "Business as Usual" (BAU) Teams
Having separate teams for "new stuff" and BAU tends to prevent learning,
improvements and ability to self-steer. It is a non-cybernetic approach.

thy for users, we can improve the kinds of interactions we have with them,
enhancing their experiences and better meeting their needs.

Increasingly, software is less of a "product for" and more of an "ongoing
conversation with" users. To make this ongoing conversation effective and successful, organizations need a "continuity of care" for its software. The team
that designs and builds the software needs to be involved in its running and
operational aspects in order to be able to build it effectively in the first place.
The team providing this "design and run" continuity of care also needs to have
some responsibility for the commercial viability of the software service; otherwise, decisions will be made in a vacuum separate from financial reality.

How can we encourage teams to continue to care about the software long
after they have finished coding a feature? One of the most important changes
to improve the continuity of care is to avoid "maintenance" or "business
as usual" (BAU) teams whose remit is simply to maintain existing software.
Sriram Narayan, author of *Agile IT Organization Design*, says "separate maintenance teams and matrix organizations...work against responsiveness."[11] By
separating the maintenance work from the initial design work, the feedback
loop from Ops to Dev is broken, and any influence that operating that software
may have on the design of the software is lost (see Figure 8.9).

Having separate teams for new-stuff and BAU also tends to prevent learning
between these two groups. The new-service team gets to implement new technologies and approaches but without any ability to see whether these approaches
are effective. The new approaches may be damaging, but the new-service

CHAPTER EIGHT

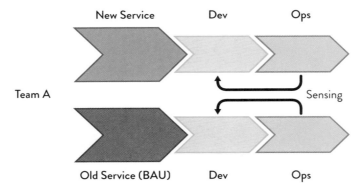

Figure 8.10: Side-by-Side New Service and BAU Teams

A cybernetic approach to maintaining older systems has a single stream-aligned team
(or pair of teams) developing and running the new service *and* the older systems,
enabling the team to retro-fit newer telemetry to the older system and increase the
fidelity of the sensing from both systems.

team has little incentive to care, as only the BAU team will feel the pain of these
poor choices. Furthermore, the BAU team typically has little chance to apply
newer telemetry techniques to existing software, leaving them blind to the signals potentially available to indicate customer happiness or unhappiness.

Instead, it is much more effective to have one team responsible for new
services and BAU of an existing system side by side. This helps the team to
increase the quality of signals from the older system by retro-fitting telemetry
from the newer system and increasing the organization's ability to sense its
environment and self steer (see Figure 8.10).

In effect, each stream-aligned team should expect to look after one or more
older systems in addition to the newer systems they are building and running.
This helps them learn about a wider range of user and system behaviors, and
avoid repeating mistakes made in earlier systems.

To generate and receive high-fidelity information from frontline, operational systems, highly skilled, highly aware people are needed. This means
that—contrary to how many IT operations teams were staffed in the past—
people in IT operations need to be able to recognize and triage problems quickly
and accurately, providing accurate, useful information to their colleagues who
are focused on building new features. Instead of the IT-operations service desk
being staffed with the most junior people, it should be staffed with some of
the most experienced engineers in the organization, either exclusively or in
tandem with some of the more junior members.

Summary: Evolving Team Topologies

The rapid pace of change in technology, markets, customer and user demands, and regulatory requirements means successful organizations need to expect to adapt and evolve their organization structure on a regular basis. However, organizations that build and run software systems need to ensure that their team interactions optimize for flow, Conway's law, and a team-first approach (including team cognitive load). By deploying the four fundamental team topologies with the three core team interaction modes, organizations gain crucial clarity of purpose for their teams on an ongoing basis. Teams understand how, when, and why they need to collaborate with other teams; how, when, and why they should be consuming or providing something "as a service"; and how, when, and why they should provide or seek facilitation with another team. Thus, an organization should expect to see different kinds of interactions between different kinds of teams at any given time as the organization responds to new challenges.

The combination of well-defined teams and well-defined interaction modes provides a powerful and flexible organizational capability for structural adaptation to changing external and internal conditions, enabling the organization to "sense" its environment, modify its activities, and focus to fit.

CHAPTER EIGHT

CONCLUSION
The Next-Generation Digital Operating Model

A second effect on performance of creating small, empowered units is to increase the likely speed of adaptation to new information.

—**John Roberts**, *The Modern Firm*

S oftware delivery in most organizations has been plagued by problems for many years—problems that new technology promises to solve but rarely (or never) does. These problems include disengaged teams, too many recurring surprises with changes in technology and markets, pushing against Conway's law, software that has grown too big for teams, a confusing array of organization design options and delivery frameworks, teams pulled in many different directions, painful reorganizations every few years, and poor flow of change. Not every organization has all of these problems, but most have some and many have almost all, despite repeated attempts to avoid them. So, what is the cause of these ongoing problems?

The reason so many organizations experience so many problems with software delivery is because most organizations have an unhelpful model of what software development is really about. An obsession with "feature delivery" ignores the human-related and team-related dynamics inherent in modern software, leading to a lack of engagement from staff, especially when the cognitive load is exceeded.

The real implications of Conway's law are almost completely ignored by most organizations, leading to, at best, happy accidents with architectural choices and, at worst, significant ongoing friction as the organization spends time and effort "fighting" the homomorphic force. Similarly, many organizations are unaware of how a poorly chosen "reorg" can destroy an organization's strategic capability for innovation and sustainable software delivery.

There is an often bewildering range of team models and scaled delivery frameworks with apparently very little to distinguish them. Furthermore, the behavior patterns of teams are rarely specified, leaving teams without clear guidelines for effective interaction with other teams, resulting in either too-tight inter-team coupling or a kind of isolationist autonomy that doesn't really scale.

Team Topologies helps to address all these points by setting forth a team-first approach to software delivery predicated on four fundamental team types, three team interaction patterns, and ways of using difficulties in delivery that empower the organization to sense its surroundings. In effect, *Team Topologies* presents a well-defined way for teams to interact and interrelate that helps to make the resulting software architecture clearer and more sustainable, turning inter-team problems into valuable signals for the self-steering organization. This is summarized in Figure 9.1:

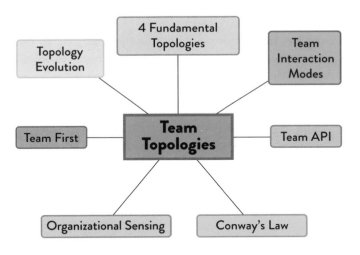

Figure 9.1: Core Ideas of Team Topologies

Four Team Types and Three Interaction Modes

Building and running a software system can be achieved using only four team types. Other team types can be actively harmful to an organization.

The four fundamental Team Topologies are:

- **Stream aligned:** a team aligned to the main flow of business change, with cross-functional skills mix and the ability to deliver significant increments without waiting on another team.
- **Platform:** a team that works on the underlying platform supporting stream-aligned teams in delivery. The platform simplifies otherwise complex technology and reduces cognitive load for teams that use it.
- **Enabling:** a team that assists other teams in adopting and modifying software as part of a transition or learning period.
- **Complicated subsystem:** a team with a special remit for a subsystem that is too complicated to be dealt with by a normal stream-aligned team or platform team. Optional and only used when really necessary.

The combination of these specific team types is all that's needed for effective software delivery with fast flow. However, the interaction modes between these four fundamental team topologies are vitally important to understanding and nurturing effective software delivery:

- **Collaboration mode:** two teams work together on a shared goal, particularly during discovery of new technology or approaches. The overhead is valuable due to the rapid pace of learning.
- **X-as-a-Service mode:** one team consumes something provided by another team (such as an API, a tool, or a full software product). Collaboration is minimal.
- **Facilitating mode:** one team (usually an enabling team) facilitates another team in learning or adopting a new approach.

Team interactions outside these three core interaction modes are wasteful and indicative of poorly chosen team responsibility boundaries and poorly understood team purposes.

Team-First Thinking: Cognitive Load, Team API, Team-Sized Architecture

To increase the clarity of purpose and define the boundary of responsibility of teams, choose a fundamental team type and an interaction mode. Team Topologies takes this "team first" approach several steps further by introducing some additional team-related guidelines that have strong outcomes for sustainable software delivery.

The Team Topologies approach treats the team as the fundamental means of delivery, where a team is not simply a collection of individuals with the same manager but an entity with its own learning, goals, mission, and reasonable autonomy. A team learns and delivers together because when this happens, the results far outperform mere collections of individuals. The team considers not just its code as part of its external "API" but also its documentation, onboarding processes, interactions with other teams in person and via chat tools, and anything else that other teams need in order to interact with its members.

To avoid software becoming ever larger and eventually overwhelming a team, the size of subsystems (or components) are limited to that manageable by a single team. Specifically, exceeding the maximum cognitive load that a team can deal with as a team is avoided, ensuring that the whole team is comfortable with the complexity and mental overheads. This "team-sized architecture" focuses on people first, and is a more sustainable and humane approach to software architecture than either monolithic or microservices architectures, both of which focus on the technology first.

Strategic Application of Conway's Law

Back in 1968, Mel Conway offered superb insight into the relationship between the communication structure of the organization and the resulting system designs, and it has become a powerful enabler (and constraint) for today's software-rich organizations: "Research which leads to techniques permitting more efficient communication among designers will play an extremely important role in the technology of system management."[1]

In today's context and terminology, the word "designers" can be replaced with "software teams." In other words, restructuring teams and facilitating (or potentially deliberately limiting) communication between teams has a much better chance of building systems that work well in production and feel natural to evolve over time. The corollary here is that increased collaboration is not always the same as increased communication. That is, if we know we need to be able to deploy different parts of the system independently, with a short lead time, and we decide to use small, decoupled services in order to do so, we need to make our teams similarly small and decoupled, with clear boundaries of responsibility.

Even performance-oriented organizations might be hindering the adoption of effective technologies and practices due to their team organization.

For instance, large, up-front designs by software architects are doomed to fail unless the designs align with the way in which the teams communicate.

Approaches to building and operating cloud software such as microservices accommodate the need for human-sized chunks of functionality alongside enhanced deployability. Teams have a greater chance of innovating and supporting a system if they can understand the constituent parts and feel a sense of ownership over the code, rather than being treated like workers on an assembly line. The use of approaches like promise theory (see Chapter 7) can help teams increase their day-to-day practical ownership of code and APIs. Organizations that develop and operate their own software systems must, therefore, set up their organizations radically differently from how it was done in the past. Team structures must match the required software architecture or risk producing unintended designs.

Evolve Organization Design for Adaptability and Sensing

Not only do organizations need to consider team structure at a single point in time, but team structures and communication pathways need to evolve with technological and organizational maturity. Periods of technical and product discovery typically require a highly collaborative environment (with fading team boundaries) to succeed. But keeping the same structures when discovery is done (established technologies and product) can lead to wasted effort and misunderstandings. In particular, organizations should expect teams to collaborate to discover new patterns and execution models, then push these down into the platform and supporting tooling.

Team Topologies is not static but capable of and expected to change as the situation changes. Multiple factors come into play when deciding which of the fundamental team topologies and interaction modes best fit the needs of the organization at a given point in time.

Team Topologies Alone Are Not Sufficient for IT Effectiveness

The Team Topologies approach to software systems represents a major step forward for many organizations around the world, providing insights into how and why different team combinations and interactions work and when to use them, along with practical advice and patterns to follow in specific circumstances.

However, Team Topologies alone will not produce an effective software-delivery and operations organization. Beyond the structures and dynamics suggested in this book, important additional ingredients of success include:

- **A healthy organizational culture:** an environment that supports the professional development of individuals and teams—one in which people feel empowered and safe to speak out about problems, and the organization expects to learn continuously.
- **Good engineering practices:** test-first design and development of all aspects of the systems, a focus on continuous delivery and operability practices, pairing and mobbing for code review, avoiding the search for a single "root cause" for incidents, designing for testability, and so on.
- **Healthy funding and financial practices:** avoiding the pernicious effects of a CapEx/OpEx split between different parts of the IT organization (or at least mitigating the worst aspects of this by estimating CapEx/OpEx through sampling the work), avoiding project-driven deadlines and large-batch budgeting wherever possible, and allocating training budgets to teams or groups rather than individuals.
- **Clarity of business vision:** the executive or leadership provides a clear, non-conflicting vision and direction for the rest of the organization, with horizons at human-relevant timescales (such as three months, six months, twelve months) and clear reasoning behind the priorities, so people in the organization can understand how and why these were chosen.

You can think of it like elements needed for creating and maintaining a garden: the Team Topologies approach acts like the instructions for placing the flowers and plants, along with patterns for pruning and training; whereas the cultural, engineering, and financial elements are like the soil, water, and fertilizer that helps the plants grow healthily.

Unhealthy cultures, poor engineering practices, and negative financial influences all act as poisons or growth inhibitors in this garden. Software cannot be expected to grow and thrive—even with excellent patterns for pruning and planting provided by Team Topologies—if the environmental conditions are hostile.

A lack of clarity in business vision is akin to asking a horticulture team to "create a garden" without any indication of the purpose of the garden. Should we grow fruit or vegetables? Should we aim for colorful flowers all year round or just in summer? Is the garden to be used for meditation or for another purpose? Likewise, clarity of purpose and vision in an organization helps to set the context for everyone in the organization to act in ways that address that purpose.

Next Steps: How to Get Started with Team Topologies

1: Start with the Team

First, as an organization ask yourself: What does the team need in order to:

- Act and operate as an effective team?
- Own part of the software effectively?
- Focus on meeting the needs of users?
- Reduce unnecessary cognitive load?
- Consume and provide software and information to other teams?

Answering these questions honestly should lead to team-first approaches to office space, developer tooling, usability of platforms, realistic subsystem/domain splitting, team-friendly architecture, rich telemetry, and so forth.

Having started with the team, you can address other important aspects of fast flow for modern software: alignment to streams, the platform, and additional capabilities to support and enhance the work of teams.

2: Identify Suitable Streams of Change

Each organization needs to choose a set of change streams that act as "pipes" down which the most important changes flow. These streams are the main focus for flow within the organization, and all other work within the organization takes place to help flow within these streams (directly or indirectly). Exactly what is chosen for the streams depends very much on the nature of the organization, but some typical streams might be:

- **Citizen-oriented tasks for government online services:** applying for a passport, paying taxes, or registering for a set of healthcare options (task-oriented streams).
- **Business banking products:** online money management, automation of bank transactions, invoicing clients (role-oriented streams).
- **Online ticket purchasing:** searching for tickets, purchasing tickets, managing "My Account" and refunds (activity streams).

- **Regional products:** European market, North American market, Asian market, etc. (geographical streams).
- **Market segment**: consumer, small and medium business, enterprise, large corporate (user-type streams).

Stream-aligned teams should be aligned to the streams you identify. These high-level streams should match the "change pressure" from the core of your organization. If there is no clear or obvious set of change streams, then it is usually beneficial to identify these before going further.

3: Identify a Thinnest Viable Platform (TVP)

After you have identified the most relevant streams for your organization, identify the services needed to support a reliable, swift flow of change in those streams. In practice, these services will form the platform on which the streams depend, but as we noted in Chapter 5, a platform does not have to be a huge, expensive investment. On the contrary, a platform can be "just big enough" to meet the flow needs for the streams: anything from a set of documentation on a wiki that helps teams use the underlying services to a full, in-house, custom-technology solution built to meet the specialist needs of the stream-aligned teams.

Naturally, the platform will evolve over time as the technology ecosystem evolves. The platform teams may start off needing to build a custom solution for, say, infrastructure provisioning, but a few years later, may discard that work in favor of a newly available, open-source or cloud-provider solution that fits better with industry trends.

Remember: technology is only ever a *part* of the platform; roadmaps, guided evolution, clear documentation, a concern for DevEx, and appropriate encapsulation of underlying complexity are all key parts of an effective delivery platform for stream-aligned teams.

4: Identify Capability Gaps in Team Coaching, Mentoring, Service Management, and Documentation

Having a team-first approach based around core streams of change enabled by a platform is a great place for an organization to start; however, the capabilities and skills needed to make this setup work are more varied and less common than many organizations expect. As we have seen in previous chapters (especially Chapter 5 and Chapter 7), you need to ensure that your teams are populated not just with technologists focused on code or computer systems but also with people who have other skills. In particular, you need people who understand and practice:

- Team coaching
- Mentoring (especially of senior staff)
- Service management (for all kinds of teams and areas, not just for production systems)
- Well-written documentation
- Process improvement

These kinds of capabilities help teams within the organization to continually improve their practices, communicate, and interact with other teams, which, in turn, helps the whole organization to safely increase the rate of change flow. No serious sports team would consider not employing coaches and trainers, and no serious organization should be without coaches and trainers either.

> We have deliberately omitted details of how to undertake large-scale transformations in an organization. For excellent patterns of organizational change, see the work of Mary Lynn Manns and Linda Rising.[2]

5: Share and Practice Different Interaction Modes and Explain Principles behind New Ways of Working

Many people have never really experienced a team-first way of working, so it will feel strange to them. Take the time to explain and demonstrate the team-interaction modes. Explain why some teams are closer together and some teams are further apart. Explain the basics of Conway's law, and how the conscious design of teams and intercommunications can help improve the software architecture of the systems being built by restricting the solution search space and saving time and effort for everyone.

Emphasize the humanistic aspects of Team Topologies: the focus on the team, the explicit limits on cognitive load, the reduction in noise and interruptions due to team-fist office space, and a limit on free-for-all communications. Identify the focus on fast flow of change for the core business streams, supported by a "thinnest viable platform" and related teams and coaching.

Above all, share how the Team Topologies approach makes for better outcomes for humans, software systems, and the organization itself.

GLOSSARY

API (application programming interface): a description and specification for how to interact programmatically with software.

application monolith: a single, large application with many dependencies and responsibilities that possibly exposes many services and/or different user journeys.

bounded context: a unit for partitioning a larger domain (or system) model into smaller parts, each of which represents an internally consistent business domain area.

Brooks's law: law coined by Fred Brooks which states that adding new people to a team doesn't immediately increase the capacity of a team.

cognitive load: the amount of working memory being used.

collaboration mode: team(s) working closely together with another team.

complicated-subsystem team: responsible for building and maintaining a part of the system that depends heavily on specialist knowledge.

Conway's law: law coined by Mel Conway that states that system design will copy the communication structures of the organization which designs it.

domain complexity: how complex the problem is that is being solved via software.

Dunbar's number: coined by anthropologist Robin Dunbar, which states that fifteen is the limit of people one person can trust; of those, only around five can be known and trusted closely.

enabling team: team(s) composed of specialists in a given technical (or product) domain; they help bridge the capability gap.

extraneous cognitive load: relates to the environment in which the task is being done (e.g., "How do I deploy this component, again?" "How do I configure this service?").

facilitating mode: team(s) helping (or being helped by) another team to clear impediments.

flow of change: a stream of related updates or alterations to a software service or system, usually aligned to user goals or other core focus of the business.

fracture plane: a natural "seam" in the software system that allows it to be easily split into two or more parts.

germane cognitive load: relates to aspects of the task that need special attention for learning or high performance (e.g., "How should this service interact with the ABC service?").

intrinsic cognitive load: relates to aspects of the task fundamental to the problem space (e.g., "What is the structure of a Java class?" "How do I create a new method?").

joined-at-the-database monolith: composed of several applications or services all coupled to the same database schema, making them difficult to change, test, and deploy separately.

monolithic build: uses one gigantic continuous integration (CI) build to get a new version of a component.

monolithic model: software that attempts to force a single domain language and representation (format) across many different contexts.

monolithic release: a set of smaller components bundled together into a "release."

monolithic thinking: "one-size-fits-all" thinking for teams that leads to unnecessary restrictions on technology and implementation approaches between teams.

monolithic workplace: a single office layout pattern for all teams and individuals in the same geographic location.

organizational sensing: teams and their internal and external communication are the "senses" of the organization (sight, sound, touch, smell, taste).

platform team: enables stream-aligned teams to deliver work with substantial autonomy.

reverse Conway maneuver: organizations should evolve their team and organizational structure to achieve the desired architecture.

stream-aligned team: a team aligned to a single, valuable stream of work.

team API: an API surrounding each team.

Team Topologies: model for organizational design that provides a key technology-agnostic mechanism for modern software-intensive enterprises to sense when a change in strategy is required (either from a business or technology point of view).

thinnest viable platform: a careful balance between keeping the platform small and ensuring that the platform is helping to accelerate and simplify software delivery for teams building on the platform.

X-as-a-Service mode: consuming or providing something with minimal collaboration.

RECOMMENDED READING

Key Management Concepts and Practices for Reliable, Fast Flow

- *Accelerate: The Science of Lean Software and DevOps: Building and Scaling High Performing Technology Organizations* by Nicole Forsgren, PhD, Jez Humble, and Gene Kim (Portland, Oregon: IT Revolution, 2018).
- *Designing Delivery: Rethinking IT in the Digital Service Economy* by Jeff Sussna (Beijing: O'Reilly Media, 2015).
- *Fearless Change: Patterns for Introducing New Ideas* by Mary Lynn Manns and Linda Rising (Boston: Addison Wesley, 2004).

Key Practices and Approaches for Organizations, Software, and Systems

- *Team Genius: The New Science of High-Performing Organizations* by Rich Karlgaard and Michael S. Malone (New York, NY: HarperBusiness, 2015).
- *Agile Development in the Large: Diving into the Deep* by Jutta Eckstein (New York: Dorset House Publishing Co Inc.,US, 2004).
- *Domain-Driven Design: Tackling Complexity in the Heart of Software* by Eric Evans (Boston: Addison-Wesley, 2003).
- *Thinking in Promises* by Mark Burgess (Sebastopol, California: O'Reilly Media, 2015).

Key Engineering Practices that Enable Fast Flow

- *Continuous Delivery: Reliable Software Releases through Build, Test, and Deployment Automation* by Jez Humble and David Farley (Upper Saddle River, NJ: Addison Wesley, 2010).

- *Release It! Design and Deploy Production-Ready Software* by Michael T. Nygard (Raleigh, North Carolina: O'Reilly, 2018).
- *Team Guide to Software Operability*, Team Guide Series 1, by Matthew Skelton and Rob Thatcher (Leeds, UK: Conflux Books, 2016).
- *Team Guide to Software Testability*, Team Guide Series 3, by Ash Winter and Rob Meaney (Leeds, UK: Conflux Books, 2018).
- *Team Guide to Software Releasability*, Team Guide Series 4, by Manuel Pais and Chris O'Dell (Leeds, UK: Conflux Books, 2018).

REFERENCES

Ackoff, Russell L. *Re-Creating the Corporation: A Design of Organizations for the 21st Century*. Oxford: Oxford University Press, 1999.

Ackoff, Russell L., Herbert J. Addison, and Sally Bibb. *Management F-Laws: How Organizations Really Work*. United Kindgom, Triarchy Press, 2007.

Adams, Paul. "Scaling Product Teams: How to Build and Structure for Hypergrowth." *Inside Intercom* (blog). January 28, 2015. https://www.intercom.com/blog/how-we-build-software/.

Adkins, Lyssa. *Coaching Agile Teams: A Companion for ScrumMasters, Agile Coaches, and Project Managers in Transition*. Upper Saddle River, NJ: Addison-Wesley Professional, 2010.

Allen, Thomas J. *Managing the Flow of Technology*. Cambridge, MA: MIT Press, 1984.

Allspaw, John. "Blameless PostMortems and a Just Culture." *Code as Craft* (blog), May 22, 2012. https://codeascraft.com/2012/05/22/blameless-postmortems/.

Almeida, Thiago. "DevOps Lessons Learned at Microsoft Engineering." *InfoQ*, May 22, 2016. https://www.infoq.com/articles/devops-lessons-microsoft.

Ancona, Deborah Gladstein, and David F. Caldwell. "Demography and Design: Predictors of New Product Team Performance." *Organization Science* 3 no. 3 (1992): 321–341. https://doi.org/10.1287/orsc.3.3.321.

Axelrod, Robert A. *Complexity of Cooperation: Agent-Based Models of Competition and Collaboration*. Princeton, NJ: Princeton University Press, 1997.

Bauernberger, Joachim. "DevOps in Telecoms—Is It Possible?" *Telecom Tech News*, October 1, 2014. http://www.telecomstechnews.com/news/2014/oct/01/devops-telecoms-it-possible/.

Beal, Helen. "The Industry Just Can't Decide about DevOps Teams." *InfoQ*, October 26, 2017. https://www.infoq.com/news/2017/10/devops-teams-good-or-bad.

Beer, Stafford. *Brain of the Firm*, 2nd edition. Chichester, UK: John Wiley & Sons, 1995.

Bennett, Drake. "The Dunbar Number, From the Guru of Social Networks." Bloomberg.com, January 11, 2013. http://www.bloomberg.com/news/articles/2013-01-10/the-dunbar-number-from-the-guru-of-social-networks.

Bernstein, Ethan, John Bunch, Niko Canner, and Michael Lee. "Beyond the Holacracy Hype." *Harvard Business Review*, July 1, 2016. https://hbr.org/2016/07/beyond-the-holacracy-hype.

Bernstein, Ethan, Jesse Shore, and David Lazer. "How Intermittent Breaks in Interaction Improve Collective Intelligence." *Proceedings of the National Academy of Sciences* 115 no. 35 (August, 2018): 8734–8739. https://doi.org/10.1073/pnas.1802407115.

Bernstein, Ethan S., and Stephen Turban. "The Impact of the 'Open' Workspace on Human Collaboration." *Philosophical Transactions of the Royal Society B* 373 no. 1753 (2018). https://doi.org/10.1098/rstb.2017.0239.

Betz, Charles. *Managing Digital: Concepts and Practices*. The Open Group, 2018.

Beyer, Betsy, Jennifer Petoff, Chris Jones, and Niall Richard Murphy (eds). *Site Reliability Engineering: How Google Runs Production Systems*. Sebastopol, CA: O'Reilly, 2016.

Blalock, Micah. "Of Mustard Seeds and Microservices." *Credera* (blog), May 6, 2015. https://www.credera.com/blog/technology-insights/java/mustard-seeds-microservices/.

Bosch, Jan. "On the Development of Software Product-Family Components." In *Software Product Lines*, edited by Robert L. Nord, 146–164. Berlin: Springer, 2004.

Bottcher, Evan. "What I Talk About When I Talk About Platforms." *MartinFowler.com* (blog), March 5, 2018. https://martinfowler.com/articles/talk-about-platforms.html.

Brandolini, Alberto. "Strategic Domain Driven Design with Context Mapping." *InfoQ*, November 25, 2009. https://www.infoq.com/articles/ddd-contextmapping.

Bright, Peter. "How Microsoft Dragged Its Development Practices into the 21st Century." *Ars Technica*, August 6, 2014. https://arstechnica.com/information-technology/2014/08/how-microsoft-dragged-its-development-practices-into-the-21st-century/.

Brooks, Fred. *The Mythical Man-Month: Essays on Software Engineering*. Boston, MA: Addison-Wesley, 1995.

Brown, Simon. "Are You a Software Architect?" *InfoQ*, February 9, 2010. https://www.infoq.com/articles/brown-are-you-a-software-architect.

Bryson, Brandon. "Architects Should Code: The Architect's Misconception." *InfoQ*, August 6, 2015. https://www.infoq.com/articles/architects-should-code-bryson.

Burgess, Mark. *Thinking in Promises: Designing Systems for Cooperation*. Sebastopol, CA: O'Reilly Media, 2015.

Carayon, Pascale. "Human Factors of Complex Sociotechnical Systems." *Applied Ergonomics, Special Issue: Meeting Diversity in Ergonomics* 37 no. 4 (2006): 525–535. https://doi.org/10.1016/j.apergo.2006.04.011.

Casella, Karen. "Improving Team Productivity by Reducing Context Switching | LinkedIn." *LinkedIn Pulse*, October 26, 2016. https://www.linkedin.com/pulse/improving-team-productivity-reducing-context-karen-casella/.

Chaudhary, Mukesh. "Working with Component Teams: How to Navigate the Complexity-Scrum Alliance." ScrumAlliance.org, September 5, 2012. https://www.scrumalliance.org/community/member-articles/301.

Cherns, Albert. "The Principles of Sociotechnical Design." *Human Relations* 29 no. 8 (1976): 783–792. https://doi.org/10.1177/001872677602900806.

Clegg, Chris W. "Sociotechnical Principles for System Design." *Applied Ergonomics* 31 no. 5 (2000): 463–477. https://doi.org/10.1016/S0003-6870(00)00009-0.

Cockcroft, Adrian. "Goto Berlin—Migrating to Microservices (Fast Delivery)." Presented at the GOTO Berlin conference, Berlin, November 15, 2014. http://www.slideshare.net/adriancockcroft/goto-berlin.

Cohn, Mike. "Nine Questions To Assess Scrum Team Structure." *Mountain Goat Software* (blog), March 9, 2010. https://www.mountaingoatsoftware.com/blog/nine-questions-to-assess-team-structure.

Conway, Melvin E. "How Do Committees Invent? Design Organization Criteria." *Datamation*, 1968.

Conway, Mel. "Toward Simplifying Application Development, in a Dozen Lessons," MelConway .com, January 3, 2017. http://melconway.com/Home/pdf/simplify.pdf.

Cooley, Faith. "Organizational Design for Effective Software Development." SlideShare, posted by Dev9Com, November 12, 2014. http://www.slideshare.net/Dev9Com/organizational -design-for-effective-software-development.

Coplien, James O., and Neil Harrison. *Organizational Patterns of Agile Software Development*. Upper Saddle River, NJ: Pearson Prentice Hall, 2005.

Cottmeyer, Mike. "Things to Consider When Structuring Your Agile Enterprise." *LeadingAgile* (blog), February 5, 2014. https://www.leadingagile.com/2014/02/structure-agile-enterprise/.

Coutu, Diane. "Why Teams Don't Work." *Harvard Business Review*, May 1, 2009. https://hbr .org/2009/05/why-teams-dont-work.

Crawford, Jason. "Amazon's 'Two-Pizza Teams': The Ultimate Divisional Organization." *JasonCrawford.org* (blog), July 30, 2013. http://blog.jasoncrawford.org/two-pizza-teams.

Cunningham, Ward. "Understand the High Cost of Technical Debt by Ward Cunningham— DZone Agile." Dzone.com, August 24, 2013. https://dzone.com/articles/understand-high -cost-technical.

Cusumano, Michael A. *Microsoft Secrets: How the World's Most Powerful Software Company Creates Technology, Shapes Markets and Manages People*, 1st Touchstone edition. New York: Simon and Schuster, 1988.

Cutler, John. "12 Signs You're Working in a Feature Factory." *Hacker Noon*, November 17, 2016. https://hackernoon.com/12-signs-youre-working-in-a-feature-factory-44a5b938d6a2.

Davies, Rachel, and Liz Sedley. *Agile Coaching*. Raleigh, NC: Pragmatic Bookshelf, 2009.

DeGrandis, Dominica. *Making Work Visible: Exposing Time Theft to Optimize Workflow*. Portland, OR: IT Revolution Press, 2017.

DeMarco, Tom, and Timothy Lister. *Peopleware: Productive Projects and Teams*, 2nd revised edition. New York, NY: Dorset, 1999.

Deming, W. Edwards. *Out of the Crisis*. Cambridge, MA: MIT Press, 1986.

DeSanctis, Gerardine, and Marshall Scott Poole. "Capturing the Complexity in Advnaced Technol- ogy Use: Adaptive Structuration Theory." *Organization Science 5* no. 2 (May 1994): 121–147.

Dogan, Jaana B. "The SRE Model." *Medium*, July 31, 2017. https://medium.com/@rakyll/the -sre-model-6e19376ef986.

Doorley, Scott, and Scott Witthoft. *Make Space: How to Set the Stage for Create Collaboration*. Hobo- ken, NJ: John Wiley & Sons, 2012.

Driskell, James E., and Eduardo Salas. "Collective Behavior and Team Performance." *Human Factors* 34 no. 3 (1992): 277–288. https://doi.org/10.1177/001872089203400303.

Driskell, James E., Eduardo Salas, and Joan Johnston. "Does Stress Lead to a Loss of Team Perspec- tive?" Group Dynamics: *Theory, Research, and Practice* 3, no. 4 (1999): 291–302.

Drucker, Peter. *The Daily Drucker: 366 Days of Insight and Motivation for Getting the Right Things Done*. New York: HarperCollins, 2018.

Dunbar, R. I. M. "Neocortex Size as a Constraint on Group Size in Primates." *Journal of Human Evo- lution* 22, no. 6 (1992): 469–493. https://doi.org/10.1016/0047-2484(92)90081-J.

Dunbar, Professor Robin. *How Many Friends Does One Person Need?: Dunbar's Number and Other Evolutionary Quirks*. London: Faber & Faber, 2010.

Eckstein, Jutta. *Agile Development in the Large: Diving into the Deep*. New York: Dorset, 2004.

Eckstein, Jutta. "Architecture in Large Scale Agile Development." In *Agile Methods. Large-Scale Development, Refactoring, Testing, and Estimation*, edited by Torgeir Dingsøyr, Nils Brede Moe, Roberto Tonelli, Steve Counsell, Cigdem Gencel, and Kai Petersen. Switzerland, Springer International Publishing, 2014.

Edmondson, Amy. "Psychological Safety and Learning Behavior in Work Teams." *Administrative Science Quarterly* 44 no. 2 (1999): 350–383. https://doi.org/10.2307/2666999.

Edmondson, Amy C. *Managing the Risk of Learning: Psychological Safety in Work Teams*. In *International Handbook of Organization Teamwork and Cooperative Working*, edited by Michael A. West, Dean Tjosvold, and Ken G. Smith. Hoboken, NJ: Wiley & Sons, 2003.

Edwards, Damon. "What is DevOps?" Dev2Ops.org, February 23, 2010. http://dev2ops org g/2010/02/what-is-devops.

The Essential Elements of Enterprise PaaS. Palo Alto, CA: Pivotal, 2015. https://content.pivotal.io /white-papers/the-essential-elements-of-enterprise-paas.

Evans, Eric. *Domain-Driven Design: Tackling Complexity in the Heart of Software*. Boston, MA: Addison Wesley, 2003.

Evans, William. "The Need for Speed: Enabling DevOps through Enterprise Architecture | #DOES16." SlideShare, posted by William Evans, November 2, 2016. https://www.slideshare. net/willevans/the-need-for-speed-enabling-devops-through-enterprise-architecture.

Fan, Xiaocong, Po-Chun Chen, and John Yen. "Learning HMM-Based Cognitive Load Models for Supporting Human-Agent Teamwork." *Cognitive Systems Research* 11, no. 1 (2010): 108–119.

Feathers, Michael. *Working Effectively with Legacy Code*. Upper Saddle River, NJ: Prentice Hall, 2004.

Forrester, Russ, and Allan B. Drexler. "A Model for Team-Based Organization Performance." *The Academy of Management Executive* 13 no. 3 (1999), 36–49.

Forsgren, PhD, Nicole, Jez Humble, and Gene Kim. *Accelerate: The Science of Lean Software and Devops: Building and Scaling High Performing Technology Organizations*. Portland, Oregon: IT Revolution Press, 2018.

Fowler, Martin. "Bliki: BoundedContext." *MartinFowler.com* (blog), January 15, 2014. https://martinfowler.com/bliki/BoundedContext.html.

Fowler, Martin. "Bliki: MicroservicePrerequisites." *MartinFowler.com* (blog), August 28, 2014. https://martinfowler.com/bliki/MicroservicePrerequisites.html.

Fried, Jason, and David Heinemeir Hansson. *Remote: Office Not Required*. NY: Crown Business, 2013.

Gothelf, Jeff, and Josh Seiden. *Sense and Respond: How Successful Organizations Listen to Customers and Create New Products Continuously*. Boston, Massachusetts: Harvard Business Review Press, 2017.

Greenleaf, Robert K. *The Servant as Leader*, Revised Edition. Atlanta, GA: The Greenleaf Center for Servant Leadership, 2015.

"Guide: Understand Team Effectiveness." re:Work website, https://rework.withgoogle.com/guides /understanding-team-effectiveness/steps/define-team/.

Hall, Jon. "ITSM, DevOps, and Why Three-Tier Support Should Be Replaced with Swarming." *Medium*, December 17, 2016. https://medium.com/@JonHall_/itsm-devops-and-why-the-three-tier-structure-must-be-replaced-with-swarming-91e76ba22304.

Hastie, Shane. "An Interview with Sam Guckenheimer on Microsoft's Journey to Cloud Cadence." *InfoQ*, October 17, 2014. https://www.infoq.com/articles/agile2014-guckenheimer.

HBS Communications. "Collaborate on Complex Problems, but Only Intermittently." *Harvard Gazette* (blog), August 15, 2018. https://news.harvard.edu/gazette/story/2018/08/collaborate-on-complex-problems-but-only-intermittently/.

Helfand, Heidi Shetzer. *Dynamic Reteaming: The Art and Wisdom of Changing Teams*. Heidi Helfand, 2018.

Hoff, Todd. "Amazon Architecture." *High Scalability* (blog), September 18, 2007. http://highscalability.com/blog/2007/9/18/amazon-architecture.html.

Holliday, Ben. "A 'Service-Oriented' Approach to Organisation Design." *FutureGov* (blog), September 25, 2018. https://blog.wearefuturegov.com/a-service-oriented-approach-to-organisation-design-1e075be7f578.

Hoskins, Drew. "What Is It like to Be Part of the Infrastructure Team at Facebook?" *Quora*, last updated February 15, 2015. https://www.quora.com/What-is-it-like-to-be-part-of-the-Infrastructure-team-at-Facebook.

Humble, Jez. "There's No Such Thing as a 'Devops Team'." *Continuous Delivery* (blog), October 19, 2012. https://continuousdelivery.com/2012/10/theres-no-such-thing-as-a-devops-team/.

Humble, Jez, and David Farley. *Continuous Delivery: Reliable Software Releases through Build, Test, and Deployment Automation*. Upper Saddle River, NJ: Addison Wesley, 2010.

Humble, Jez, Joanne Molesky, and Barry O'Reilly. *Lean Enterprise: How High Performance Organizations Innovate at Scale*. Sebastopol, CA: O'Reilly Media, 2015.

Ilgen, Daniel R., and John R. Hollenbeck. 'Effective Team Performance under Stress and Normal Conditions: An Experimental Paradigm, Theory and Data for Studying Team Decision Making in Hierarchical Teams with Distributed Expertise'. DTIC Document, 1993. http://oai.dtic.mil/oai/oai?verb=getRecord&metadataPrefix=html&identifier=ADA284683.

Ingles, Paul. "Convergence to Kubernetes." *Paul Ingles* (blog), June 18, 2018. https://medium.com/@pingles/convergence-to-kubernetes-137ffa7ea2bc.

innolution. n.d. "Feature Team Definition | Innolution." Accessed October 14, 2018. https://innolution.com/resources/glossary/feature-team

"DevOps Over Coffee—Adidas." YouTube video, 32:03, posted by IT Revolution, July 3, 2018. https://www.youtube.com/watch?v=oOjdXeGp44E&feature=youtu.be&t=1071.

Jang, Sujin. "Cultural Brokerage and Creative Performance in Multicultural Teams." *Organization Science* 28 no. 6 (2017): 993–1009. https://doi.org/10.1287/orsc.2017.1162.

Jay, Graylin, Joanne Hale, Randy Smith, David Hale, Nicholas Kraft, and Charles Ward. "Cyclomatic Complexity and Lines of Code: Empirical Evidence of a Stable Linear Relationship." *Journal of Software Engineering & Applications* 2 (January): 137–143. https://doi.org/10.4236/jsea.2009.23020.

John, Wolfgang. "DevOps for Service Providers—Next Generation Tools." *Ericsson Research Blog*. December 7, 2015. https://www.ericsson.com/research-blog/cloud/devops-for-service-providers-next-generation-tools/.

Johnston, Joan H., Stephen M. Fiore, Carol Paris, and C. A. P. Smith. "Application of Cognitive Load Theory to Developing a Measure of Team Decision Efficiency." *Military Psychology* 3 (2003). https://www.tandfonline.com/doi/abs/10.1037/h0094967.

Karlgaard, Rich, and Michael S. Malone. *Team Genius: The New Science of High-Performing Organizations*. New York, NY: HarperBusiness, 2015.

Kelly, Allan. *Business Patterns for Software Developers*. Chichester, UK: John Wiley & Sons, 2012.

Kelly, Allan. "Conway's Law v. Software Architecture." Dzone.com (blog), March 14, 2013. https://dzone.com/articles/conways-law-v-software.

Kelly, Allan. "Conway's Law & Continuous Delivery." SlideShare, posted by Allen Kelly, April 9, 2014, https://www.slideshare.net/allankellynet/conways-law-continuous-delivery.

Kelly, Allan. "No Projects—Beyond Projects." *InfoQ*, December 5, 2014. https://www.infoq.com/articles/kelly-beyond-projects.

Kelly, Allan. *Project Myopia: Why Projects Damage Software #NoProjects*. Allan Kelly: 2018.

Kelly, Allan. "Return to Conway's Law." *Allan Kelly Associates* (blog), January 17, 2006. https://www.allankellyassociates.co.uk/archives/1169/return-to-conways-law/.

Kersten, Mik. *Project to Product: How to Survive and Thrive in the Age of Digital Disruption with the Flow Framework*. Portland, OR: IT Revolution Press, 2018.

Kim, Gene, Jez Humble, Patrick Debois, and John Willis. *The DevOps Handbook: How to Create World-Class Agility, Reliability, and Security in Technology Organizations*. Portland, OR: IT Revolution Press, 2016.

Kim, Dr. Kyung Hee, and Robert A. Pierce. "Convergent Versus Divergent Thinking." In *Encyclopedia of Creativity, Invention, Innovation and Entrepreneurship*, edited by Elias G. Carayannis, 245–250. New York: Springer, 2013.

Kitagawa, Justin. "Platforms at Twilio: Unlocking Developer Effectiveness." *InfoQ*, October 18, 2018. https://www.infoq.com/presentations/twilio-devops

Kitson, Jon. "Squad Health Checks." *Sky Betting & Gaming Technology* (blog), February 1, 2017. https://technology.skybettingandgaming.com/2017/02/01/squad-health-checks/.

Kniberg, Henrik, and Anders Ivarsson. "Scaling Agile @ Spotify with Tribes, Squads, Chapters & Guilds." *Crisp's Blog*. October 2012. https://blog.crisp.se/wp-content/uploads/2012/11/SpotifyScaling.pdf.

Kniberg, Henrik. "Real-Life Agile Scaling." Presented at the Agile Tour Bangkok, Thailand, November 21, 2015. http://blog.crisp.se/wp-content/uploads/2015/11/Real-life-agile-scaling.pdf.

Kniberg, Henrik. "Squad Health Check Model—Visualizing What to Improve." *Spotify Labs* (blog), September 16, 2014. https://labs.spotify.com/2014/09/16/squad-health-check-model/

Knight, Pamela. "Acquisition Community Team Dynamics: The Tuckman Model vs. the DAU Model." *Proceedings from the 4th Annual Acquisition Research Symposium of the Naval Postgraduate School* (2007). https://apps.dtic.mil/dtic/tr/fulltext/u2/a493549.pdf.

Kotter, John P. "Accelerate!" *Harvard Business Review*, November 1, 2012. https://hbr.org/2012/11/accelerate.

Kramer, Staci D. "The Biggest Thing Amazon Got Right: The Platform." *Gigaom*, October 12, 2011. https://gigaom.com/2011/10/12/419-the-biggest-thing-amazon-got-right-the-platform/.

Laloux, Frédéric. *Reinventing Organizations: An Illustrated Invitation to Join the Conversation on Next-Stage Organizations*. Oxford, UK: Nelson Parker, 2016.

Lane, Kim. "The Secret to Amazon's Success—Internal APIs." *API Evangelist* (blog), January 12, 2012. http://apievangelist.com/2012/01/12/the-secret-to-amazons-success-internal-apis/.

Larman, Craig, and Bas Vodde. "Choose Feature Teams over Component Teams for Agility." *InfoQ*, July 15, 2008. https://www.infoq.com/articles/scaling-lean-agile-feature-teams.

Larman, Craig, and Bas Vodde. *Large-Scale Scrum: More with LeSS*. Upper Saddle River, NJ: Addison-Wesley Professional, 2016.

Leffingwell, Dean. "Feature Teams vs. Component Teams (Continued)." *Scaling Software Agility* (blog), May 2, 2011. https://scalingsoftwareagility.wordpress.com/2011/05/02/feature-teams-vs-component-teams-continued/.

Leffingwell, Dean. "Organizing at Scale: Feature Teams vs. Component Teams – Part 3." *Scaling Software Agility* (blog), July 22, 2009. https://scalingsoftwareagility.wordpress.com/2009/07/22/organizing-agile-at-scale-feature-teams-versus-component-teams-part-3/.

Leffingwell, Dean. *Scaling Software Agility: Best Practices for Large Enterprises*. Upper Saddle River, NJ: Addison-Wesley Professional, 2007.

Lencioni, Patrick M. *The Five Dysfunctions of a Team: A Leadership Fable*. San Francisco, CA: John Wiley & Sons, 2002.

Leveson, Nancy G. *Engineering a Safer World: Systems Thinking Applied to Safety*. Cambridge, MA: MIT Press, 2017.

Levina, Natalia, and Emmanuelle Vaast. "The Emergence of Boundary Spanning Competence in Practice: Implications for Information Systems' Implementation and Use." *MIS Quarterly* 29 no. 2 (June 2005): 335–363. https://papers.ssrn.com/abstract=1276022.

Lewis, James. "Microservices and the Inverse Conway Manoeuvre—James Lewis." YouTube video, 57:57, posted by NDC Conferences, February 16, 2017. https://www.youtube.com/watch?v=uamh7xppO3E.

Lim, Beng-Chong, and Katherine J. Klein. "Team Mental Models and Team Performance: A Field Study of the Effects of Team Mental Model Similarity and Accuracy." *Journal of Organizational Behavior* 27, no. 4 (June 1, 2006): 403–418. https://doi.org/10.1002/job.387.

Linders, Ben. "Scaling Teams to Grow Effective Organizations." *InfoQ*, August 11, 2016. https://www.infoq.com/news/2016/08/scaling-teams.

Long, Josh. "GARY (Go Ahead, Repeat Yourself)." Tweet @starbuxman, May 25, 2016. https://twitter.com/starbuxman/status/735550836147814400.

Lowe, Steven A. "How to Use Event Storming to Achieve Domain-Driven Design." *TechBeacon*, October 15, 2015. https://techbeacon.com/introduction-event-storming -easy-way-achieve-domain-driven-design.

Luo, Jiao, Andrew H. Van de Ven, Runtian Jing, and Yuan Jiang. "Transitioning from a Hierarchical Product Organization to an Open Platform Organization: A Chinese Case Study." *Journal of Organization Design* 7 (January): 1. https://doi.org/10.1186/s41469-017-0026-x.

MacCormack, Alan, John Rusnak, and Carliss Y. Baldwin. "Exploring the Structure of Complex Software Designs: An Empirical Study of Open Source and Proprietary Code." *Management Science* 52, no. 7 (2006): 1015–1030. https://doi.org/10.1287/mnsc.1060.0552.

MacCormack, Alan, Carliss Y. Baldwin, and John Rusnak. "Exploring the Duality Between Product and Organizational Architectures: A Test of the 'Mirroring' Hypothesis." *Research Policy* 41, no. 8 (October 2012): 1309–1024. http://www.hbs.edu/faculty/Pages/item.aspx?num=43260.

REFERENCES

Malan, Ruth. "Conway's Law." *TraceintheSand.com* (blog), February 13, 2008. http://traceinthe
sand.com/blog/2008/02/13/conways-law/.

Manns, Mary Lynn, and Linda Rising, *Fearless Change: Patterns for Introducing New Ideas.* Boston, MA: Addison Wesley, 2004.

Marshall, Bob. "A Team Is Not a Group of People Who Work Together. A Team Is a Group of People Who Each Put the Team before Themselves." Tweet, @flowchainsensei, October 29, 2018. https://twitter.com/flowchainsensei/status/1056838136574152704.

McChrystal, General Stanley, David Silverman, Tantum Collins, and Chris Fussell. *Team of Teams: New Rules of Engagement for a Complex World.* New York, NY: Portfolio Penguin, 2015.

Meadows, Donella. *Leverage Points: Places to Intervene in a System.* Hartland, VT: Sustainability Institute, 1999. http://donellameadows.org/wp-content/userfiles/Leverage_Points.pdf.

"Microservices: Organizing Large Teams for Rapid Delivery." SlideShare, posted by Pivotal, August 10, 2016. https://www.slideshare.net/Pivotal/microservices-organizing-large-teams -for-rapid-delivery.

Mihaljov, Timo. "Having a Dedicated DevOps Person Who Does All the DevOpsing Is like Having a Dedicated Collaboration Person Who Does All the Collaborating." Tweet. @noidi. April 14, 2017. https://twitter.com/noidi/status/852879869998501889.

Miller, G. A. "The Magical Number Seven, Plus or Minus Two: Some Limits on Our Capacity for Processing Information." *Psychological Review* 63 no. 2 (1956): 81–97.

Minick, Eric. "The Goal for a 'DevOps Team' Should Be to Put Itself out of Business by Enabling the Rest of the Org." Tweet, @ericminick, October 8, 2014. https://twitter.com/ericminick /status/517335119330172930.

Minick, Eric, and Curtis Yanko. "Creating a DevOps Team That Isn't Evil." SlideShare, posted by IBM Urban Code Products, March 5, 2015. http://www.slideshare.net/Urbancode /creating-a-devops-team-that-isnt-evil.

Mole, David. "Drive: How We Used Daniel Pink's Work to Create a Happier, More Productive Work Place." *InfoQ*, September 10, 2015. https://www.infoq.com/articles/drive-productive -workplace.

Morgan-Smith, Victoria, and Matthew Skelton. *Internal Tech Conferences.* Leeds, UK: Conflux Digital, 2019.

Morris, Kief. *Infrastructure as Code: Managing Servers in the Cloud.* Sebastopol, CA: O'Reilly Media, 2016.

Munns, Chris. "Chris Munns, DevOps @ Amazon: Microservices, 2 Pizza Teams, & 50 Million Deploys per Year." SlideShare.net, posted by TriNimbus, May 6, 2016. http://www.slideshare .net/TriNimbus/chris-munns-devops-amazon-microservices-2-pizza-teams-50-million -deploys-a-year.

Murphy, Niall. "What is 'Site Reliability Engineering'?" Landing.Google.com, https://landing .google.com/sre/interview/ben-treynor.html.

Murphy, Niall and Ben Treynor. "What is 'Site Reliability Engineering'?" Landing.Google.com (blog), accessed March 21, 2019. https://landing.google.com/sre/interview/ben-treynor .html.

Narayan, Sriram. *Agile IT Organization Design: For Digital Transformation and Continuous Delivery.* New York: Addison-Wesley Professional, 2015.

Neumark, Peter. "DevOps & Product Teams—Win or Fail?" *InfoQ*, June 29, 2015. https://www
.infoq.com/articles/devops-product-teams.

Netflix Technology Blog. "Full Cycle Developers at Netflix—Operate What You Build." *Medium
.com*, May 17, 2018, https://medium.com/netflix-techblog/full-cycle-developers-at-netflix
-a08c31f83249.

Netflix Technology Blog. "The Netflix Simian Army." Netflix TechBlog, July 19, 2011. https://
medium.com/netflix-techblog/the-netflix-simian-army-16e57fbab116.

Newman, Sam. *Building Microservices: Design Fine-Grained Systems*. Sebastopol, CA: O'Reilly Media,
2015.

Newman, Sam. "Demystifying Conway's Law." ThoughtWorks (blog) June 30, 2014. https://www
.thoughtworks.com/insights/blog/demystifying-conways-law.

Nygard, Michael. "The Perils of Semantic Coupling—Wide Awake Developers." MichaelNygard
.com (blog), April 29, 2015. http://michaelnygard.com/blog/2015/04/the-perils-of
-semantic-coupling/.

Nygard, Michael T. *Release It! Design and Deploy Production-Ready Software*, 2nd edition. Raleigh,
North Carolina: O'Reilly, 2018.

O'Connor, Debra L., and Tristan E. Johnson. "Understanding Team Cognition in Performance
Improvement Teams: A Meta-Analysis of Change in Shared Mental Models." *Proceedings of
the Second International Conference on Concept Mapping* (2006). https://pdfs.semanticscholar
.org/4106/3eb1567e630a35b4f33f281a6bb9d193ddf5.pdf.

O'Dell, Chris. "You Build It, You Run It (Why Developers Should Also Be on Call)." Skelton
Thatcher.com (blog), October 18, 2017. https://skeltonthatcher.com/blog/build-run
-developers-also-call/.

Overeem, Barry. "How I Used the Spotify Squad Health Check Model—Barry Overeem—The
Liberators." BarryOvereem.com (blog), August 7, 2015. http://www.barryovereem.com
/how-i-used-the-spotify-squad-health-check-model/.

Pais, Manuel. "Damon Edwards: DevOps is an Enterprise Concern" *InfoQ*, May 31, 2014. https://
www.infoq.com/interviews/interview-damon-edwards-qcon-2014.

Pais, Manuel. "Prezi's CTO on How to Remain a Lean Startup after 4 Years." *InfoQ*, October 5, 2012.
https://www.infoq.com/news/2012/10/Prezi-lean-startup.

Pais, Manuel, and Matthew Skelton. "The Divisive Effect of Separate Issue Tracking Tools." *InfoQ*,
March 22, 2017. https://www.infoq.com/articles/issue-tracking-tools.

Pais, Manuel, and Matthew Skelton. "Why and How to Test Logging." *InfoQ*, October 29, 2016.
https://www.infoq.com/articles/why-test-logging.

Pearce, Jo. "Day 3: Managing Cognitive Load for Team Learning." *12 Devs of Xmas* (blog),
December 28, 2015. http://12devsofxmas.co.uk/2015/12/day-3-managing-cognitive-load
-for-team-learning/.

Pearce, Jo. "Hacking Your Head : Managing Information Overload (Extended)." SlideShare,
posted by Jo Pearce, April 29, 2016. https://www.slideshare.net/JoPearce5/hacking-your
-head-managing-information-overload-extended.

Perri, Melissa. *Escaping the Build Trap: How Effective Product Management Creates Real Value*. Sebastopol, CA: O'Reilly, 2018.

Pflaeging, Niels. *Organize for Complexity: How to Get Life Back Into Work to Build the High-Performance
Organization*, 1st edition. Germany: BetaCodex Publishing, 2014.

Pflaeging, Niels. "Org Physics: The 3 Faces of Every Company." *Niels Pflaeging* (blog), March 6, 2017. https://medium.com/@NielsPflaeging/org-physics-the-3-faces-of-every-company-df16025f65f8.

Phillips, Amy. "Testing Observability." *InfoQ*, April 5, 2018. https://www.infoq.com/presentations/observability-testing.

Pink, Daniel. *Drive: The Surprising Truth About What Motivates Us.* New York: Riverhead Books, 2009.

Raymond, Eric. *The New Hacker's Dictionary*, 3rd Edition. Boston, MA: MIT Press, 1996.

Reed, J. Paul. "Blameless Postmortems Don't Work. Be Blame-Aware but Don't Go Negative." *TechBeacon*, March 22, 2016. https://techbeacon.com/blameless-postmortems-dont-work-heres-what-does.

Reinertsen, Donald. *The Principles of Product Development Flow: Second Generation Lean Product Development.* Redondo Beach, CA: Celeritas Publishing, 2009.

Rensin, Dave. "Introducing Google Customer Reliability Engineering." Google Cloud Blog, October 10, 2016. https://cloud.google.com/blog/products/gcp/introducing-a-new-era-of-customer-support-google-customer-reliability-engineering/.

Roberts, John. *The Modern Firm: Organizational Design for Performance and Growth.* Oxford: Oxford University Press, 2007.

Robertson, Brian J. *Holocracy: The New Management System for a Rapidly Changing World.* NY: Henry Holt, 2015.

Rock, David, and Heidi Grant. *Why Diverse Teams Are Smarter.* Cambridge, MA: Harvard Business Review, 2016.

Rother, Mike. *Toyota Kata: Managing People for Improvement, Adaptiveness and Superior Results.* New York: McGraw-Hill Education, 2009.

Rozovsky, Julia. "Re:Work—The Five Keys to a Successful Google Team." re:Work (blog), November 17, 2015. https://rework.withgoogle.com/blog/five-keys-to-a-successful-google-team/.

Rubin, Kenneth S. *Essential Scrum: A Practical Guide to the Most Popular Agile Process.* Upper Saddle River, NJ: Addison Wesley, 2012.

Rummler, Geary, and Alan Brache. *Improving Performance: How to Manage the White Space on the Organization Chart*, 3rd edition. San Francisco, CA: Jossey-Bass, 2013.

Salas, Eduardo, and Stephen M. Fiore, eds. *Team Cognition: Understanding the Factors That Drive Process and Performance.* Washington, DC: American Psychological Association, 2004.

Scholtes, Ingo, Pavlin Mavrodiev, and Frank Schweitzer. "From Aristotle to Ringelmann: A Large-Scale Analysis of Team Productivity and Coordination in Open Source Software Projects." *Empirical Software Engineering* 21 no. 2 (2016): 642–683. https://doi.org/10.1007/s10664-015-9406-4.

Schotkamp, Tom, and Martin Danoesastro. "HR's Pioneering Role in Agile at ING." *BCG* (blog), June 1, 2018. https://www.bcg.com/en-gb/publications/2018/human-resources-pioneering-role-agile-ing.aspx.

Schwartz, Mark, Jason Cox, Jonathan Snyder, Mark Rendell, Chivas Nambiar, and Mustafa Kapadia. *Thinking Environments: Evaluating Organization Models for DevOps to Accelerate.* Portland, OR: IT Revolution Press, 2016.

Seiter, Courtney. "We've Changed Our Product Team Structure 4 Times: Here's Where We Are Today." *Buffer* (blog), October 20, 2015. https://open.buffer.com/product-team-evolution/.

Shibata, Kenichi. "How to Build a Platform Team Now! The Secrets to Successful Engineering." *Hacker Noon* (blog), September 29, 2018. https://hackernoon.com/how-to-build-a-platform-team -now-the-secrets-to-successful-engineering-8a9b6a4d2c8.

Simenon, Stefan, and Wiebe de Roos. "Transforming CI/CD at ABN AMRO to Accelerate Software Delivery and Improve Security." SlideShare, posted by DevOps.com, March 27, 2018. https://www.slideshare.net/DevOpsWebinars/transforming-cicd-at-abn-amro-to -accelerate-software-delivery-and-improve-security.

Sinha, Harsh. "Harsh Sinha on Building Culture at TransferWise." *InfoQ*, February 19, 2018. https://www.infoq.com/podcasts/Harsh-Sinha-transferwise-building-culture.

Skelton, Matthew. "How Different Team Topologies Influence DevOps Culture." *InfoQ*, September 2, 2015. https://www.infoq.com/articles/devops-team-topologies.

Skelton, Matthew. "How to Find the Right DevOps Tools for Your Team." *TechBeacon*, 2018. https:// techbeacon.com/how-find-right-devops-tools-your-team.

Skelton, Matthew. "Icebreaker for Agile Retrospectives—Empathy Snap." MatthewSkelton.net (blog), November 15, 2012. http://empathysnap.com/.

Skelton, Matthew. *Tech Talks for Beginners*. Leeds, UK: Conflux Digital, 2018.

Skelton, Matthew. "What Team Structure Is Right for DevOps to Flourish?" Matthew Skelton.net (blog), October 22, 2013. https://blog.matthewskelton.net/2013/10/22/what -team-structure-is-right-for-devops-to-flourish/.

Skelton, Matthew. "Your Team's API Includes: - Code: REST Endpoints, Libraries, Clients, UI, Etc.—Wiki / Docs—Especially 'How To' Guides—Your Approach to Team Chat Tools (Slack /Hipchat)—Anything Else Which Other Teams Need to Use to Interact with Your Team It's Not Just about Code. #DevEx." Tweet, @matthewpskelton, July 25, 2018. https://twitter .com/matthewpskelton/status/1022111880423395329.

Skelton, Matthew, and Rob Thatcher. *Team Guide to Software Operability*. Leeds, UK: Conflux Books, 2016.

Skulmowski, Alexander, and Rey, Günter Daniel. "Measuring Cognitive Load in Embodied Learning Settings." *Frontiers in Psychology* 8 (August 2, 2017). https://doi.org/10.3389 /fpsyg.2017.01191.

Smith, Steve, and Matthew Skelton, eds. *Build Quality In*. Leeds, UK: Conflux Digital, 2015.

Snowden, Dave. "The Rule of 5, 15 & 150." Cognitive Edge (blog), December 10, 2006. http:// cognitive-edge.com/blog/logn-0-093-3-389-logcr-1-r20-764-t3410-35-p0-001/.

Sosa, Manuel E., Steven D. Eppinger, and Craig M. Rowles. "The Misalignment of Product Architecture and Organizational Structure in Complex Product Development." *Management Science* 50 no. 12 (December 2004): 1674–1689.

Stanford, Naomi. *Guide to Organisation Design: Creating High-Performing and Adaptable Enterprises (Economist Books)*, 2nd Edition. London: Economist Books, 2015.

Stompff, Guido. "Facilitating Team Cognition: How Designers Mirror What NPD Teams Do." *ResearchGate*, September 2012. https://www.researchgate.net/publication/254831689 _Facilitating_Team_Cognition_How_designers_mirror_what_NPD_teams_do.

Strode, Diane E., Sid L. Huff, Beverley Hope, and Sebastian Link. "Coordination in Co-Located Agile Software Development Projects." *Journal of Systems and Software, Special Issue: Agile Development* 85, no. 6 (June 1, 2012): 1222–38. https://doi.org/10.1016/j.jss.2012.02.017.

Sussna, Jeff. *Designing Delivery: Rethinking IT in the Digital Service Economy*. Sebastopol, CA: O'Reilly Media, 2015.

Sweller, John. "Cognitive Load During Problem Solving: Effects on Learning." *Cognitive Science* 12 no. 2 (1988): 257–285.

Sweller, John. "Cognitive Load Theory, Learning Difficulty, and Instructional Design." *Learning and Instruction* 4 (1994): 295–312.

"System Team." Scaled Agile Framework website, last updated October 5, 2018. https://www.scaledagileframework.com/system-team/.

Tuckman, Bruce W. "Developmental Sequence in Small Groups." *Psychological Bulletin* 63 no. 6 (1965): 384–399. https://doi.org/10.1037/h0022100.

Tune, Nick. "Domain-Driven Architecture Diagrams." *Nick Tune's Tech Strategy Blog*, August 15, 2015. https://medium.com/nick-tune-tech-strategy-blog/domain-driven-architecture-diagrams-139a75acb578.

Tune, Nick, and Scott Millett. *Designing Autonomous Teams and Services*. Sebastopol, CA: O'Reilly Media, 2017.

Urquhart, James. "Communications and Conway's Law." *Digital Anatomy* (blog), September 28, 2016. https://medium.com/digital-anatomy/communications-and-conways-law-6a1a9deae32.

Urquhart, James. "IT Operations in a Cloudy World." *CNET*, September 15, 2010. https://www.cnet.com/news/it-operations-in-a-cloudy-world/.

Wardley, Simon. "An Introduction to Wardley 'Value Chain' Mapping." *CIO UK*, March 19, 2015. https://www.cio.co.uk/it-strategy/introduction-wardley-value-chain-mapping-3604565/.

Wastell, Katherine. "What We Mean When We Talk about Service Design at the Co-Op." Co-Op Digital Blog, October 25, 2018. https://digitalblog.coop.co.uk/2018/10/25/what-we-mean-when-we-talk-about-service-design-at-the-co-op/.

Webber, Emily. *Building Successful Communities of Practice*. San Francisco, CA: Blurb, 2018.

Weinberg, Gerald M. *An Introduction to General Systems Thinking, 25th Silver Anniversary Edition*. New York: Dorset, 2001.

Wiener, Norbert. *Cybernetics: Or Control and Communication in the Animal and the Machine*, 2nd edition. Cambridge, Mass: MIT Press, 1961.

Westrum, R. 2004. "A Typology of Organisational Cultures." *Quality & Safety in Health Care* 13 Suppl. 2 (1961): ii22–27. https://doi.org/10.1136/qshc.2003.009522.

"What Team Structure is Right for DevOps to Flourish?" DevOpsTopologies.com, accessed March 21, 2019. http://web.devopstopologies.com.

Wiley, Evan. "Scaling XP Through Self-Similarity at Pivotal Cloud Foundry." *Agile Alliance* (blog), July 28, 2018. https://www.agilealliance.org/resources/experience-reports/scaling-xp-through-self-similarity-at-pivotal-cloud-foundry/.

Womack, James P., and Daniel T. Jones. *Lean Thinking: Banish Waste and Create Wealth In Your Corporation*. NY: Simon & Schuster/Free Press, 2003.

Zambonelli, Franco. "Toward Sociotechnical Urban Superorganisms." *Computer*, 2012. http://spartan.ac.brocku.ca/~tkennedy/COMM/Zambonelli2012.pdf.

NOTES

Foreword

1. Conway, "How Do Committees Invent?."

Preface

1. Skelton, "What Team Structure Is Right for DevOps to Flourish?"
2. Skelton, "How Different Team Topologies Influence DevOps Culture."

Chapter 1

1. Schwartz et al., *Thinking Environments*, 21.
2. Pflaeging, *Organize for Complexity*, 34–41.
3. Pflaeging, *Organize for Complexity*.
4. Laloux, *Reinventing Organizations*; Robertson, *Holocracy*.
5. Stanford, *Guide to Organisation Design*, 14–16.
6. Conway, "How do Committees Invent?, 31.
7. Conway, "How do Committees Invent?"; Kelly, "Conway's Law & Continuous Delivery."
8. Kelly, "Conway's Law v. Software Architecture."
9. Raymond, *The New Hacker's Dictionary*, 124.
10. Lewis, "Microservices and the Inverse Conway."
11. Pink, *Drive*, 49.

Chapter 2

1. "DevOps Over Coffee – Adidas;" Fernando Cornago, person email communication with the authors, March 2019.
2. MacCormack et al., "Exploring the Structure of Complex Software Designs," 1015–1030; MacCormack et al., "Exploring the Duality Between Product and Organizational Architectures," 1309–1024.
3. Sosa et al., "The Misalignment of Product Architecture and Organizational Structure in Complex Product Development," 1674–1689.
4. Malan, "Conway's Law."
5. Conway, "How do Committees Invent?" 28.
6. Forsgren et al., *Accelerate*, 63.
7. Nygard, *Release It!*, 4.
8. MacCormack et al., "Exploring the Structure of Complex Software Designs."
9. Roberts, *The Modern Firm*, 190.
10. Reinertsen, *The Principles of Product Development Flow*, 257.
11. Malan, "Conway's Law."
12. Kelly, "Return to Conway's Law."

13. Stanford, *Guide to Organisation Design*, 4.
14. Sosa et al., "The Misalignment of Product Architecture."
15. Cohn, "Nine Questions to Assess Scrum Team Structure."
16. Kniberg, "Real-Life Agile Scaling."

Chapter 3

1. Driskell and Salas, "Collective Behavior and Team Performance," 277–288.
2. McChrystal et al., *Team of Teams*, 94.
3. Rozovsky, "Re:Work—The Five Keys to a Successful Google Team."
4. Crawford, At opening quotes. "Amazon's 'Two-Pizza Teams.'"
5. Dunbar, "Neocortex Size as a Constraint on Group Size in Primates," 469–493.
6. Snowden, "The Rule of 5, 15 & 150;" Dunbar, *How Many Friends Does One Person Need?*; Bennett, "The Dunbar Number, From the Guru of Social Networks;" Burgess, *Thinking in Promises*, 87.
7. Snowden, "The Rule of 5, 15 & 150;" Karlgaard and Malone, *Team Genius*, 201–205.
8. Lewis, "Microservices and the Inverse Conway Manoeuvre."
9. Munns, "Chris Munns, DevOps @ Amazon."
10. Brooks, *The Mythical Man-Month*.
11. Tuckman, "Developmental Sequence in Small Groups," 384–399.
12. Kelly, *Project Myopia*, 72.
13. Helfand, *Dynamic Reteaming*, 123.
14. Knight, "Acquisition Community Team Dynamics."
15. Humble et al., *Lean Enterprise*, 37.
16. Driskell and Salas, "Collective Behavior and Team Performance;" Rock and Grant, *Why Diverse Teams Are Smarter*.
17. Jang, "Cultural Brokerage and Creative Performance in Multicultural Teams," 993–1009; Carayon, "Human Factors of Complex Sociotechnical Systems," 525–535.
18. DeMarco and Lister, *Peopleware*, 156.
19. Stanford, *Guide to Organisation Design*, 287.
20. Deming, *Out of the Crisis*, 22.
21. Roberts, *The Modern Firm*, 277.
22. Sweller, "Cognitive Load During Problem Solving: Effects on Learning," 257–285.
23. Pearce, "Day 3: Managing Cognitive Load for Team Learning;" Pearce, "Hacking Your Head."
24. Driskell et al., "Does Stress Lead to a Loss of Team Perspective," 300.
25. Jay et al., "Cyclomatic Complexity and Lines of Code," 137–143.
26. MacChrystal et al., *Team of Teams*, 94.
27. Lim and Klein, "Team Mental Models and Team Performance," 403–418.
28. Evan Wiley, as quoted in Helfand, *Dynamic Reteaming*, 121.
29. Jeff Bezos, as quoted in Lane, "The Secret to Amazon's Success."
30. Axelrod, *Complexity of Cooperation*; Burgess, *Thinking in Promises*, 73.
31. Kniberg and Ivarsson, "Scaling Agile @ Spotify."
32. Kniberg and Ivarsson, "Scaling Agile @ Spotify."
33. Forsgren et al., *Accelerate*, 181.
34. Jeremy Brown, personal communication with the authors, March 2019.
35. Doorley and Witthoft, *Make Space*, 16.
36. Fried and Hansson, *Remote*, 91.

Chapter 4

1. Stanford, *Guide to Organisation Design*, 3.
2. Kniberg and Ivarsson, "Scaling Agile @ Spotify."

3. Kniberg and Ivarsson, "Scaling Agile @ Spotify."
4. Kniberg and Ivarsson, "Scaling Agile @ Spotify."
5. Forsgren et al., *Accelerate*, 63.
6. Skelton, "What Team Structure Is Right for DevOps to Flourish?"
7. John, "DevOps for Service Providers—Next Generation Tools."
8. Hastie, "An Interview with Sam Guckenheimer on Microsoft's Journey to Cloud Cadence."
9. Ben Treynor, as quoted in Niall Murphy, "What is 'Site Reliability Engineering'?"
10. Dogan, "The SRE Model."
11. Rensin, "Introducing Google Customer Reliability Engineering."
12. Netflix Technology Blog, "Full Cycle Developers at Netflix—Operate What You Build."
13. DeGrandis, *Making Work Visible*, 82.
14. Strode and Huff, "A Taxonomy of Dependencies in Agile Software Development."
15. Pulak Agrawal, personal communication with the authors, March 2019.
16. Pulak Agrawal, personal communication with the authors, March 2019.

Chapter 5

1. Luo et al., "Transitioning from a Hierarchical Product Organization to an Open Platform Organization."
2. Reinertsen, *The Principles of Product Development Flow*, 265.
3. Lane, "The Secret to Amazon's Success—Internal APIs;" Hoff, "Amazon Architecture."
4. Crawford, "Amazon's 'Two-Pizza Teams;'" Munns, "Chris Munns, DevOps @ Amazon."
5. Kramer, "The Biggest Thing Amazon Got Right."
6. Sussna, *Designing Delivery*, 148.
7. Pink, *Drive*, 49.
8. Eckstein, "Architecture in Large Scale Agile Development," 21–29.
9. Robert Greenleaf, *The Servant as Leader*.
10. DeMarco and Lister, *Peopleware*, 212.
11. Webber, *Building Successful Communities of Practice*, 11.
12. Bottcher, "What I Talk About When I Talk About Platforms."
13. Eckstein, *Agile Development in the Large*, 53.
14. Neumark, "DevOps & Product Teams—Win or Fail?"
15. Reinertsen, *The Principles of Product Development Flow*, 292.
16. Womack and Jones, *Lean Thinking*.
17. Urquhart, "IT Operations in a Cloudy World."
18. Kniberg, "Real-Life Agile Scaling."
19. Kelly, *Business Patterns for Software Developers*, 88–89.
20. Conway, "Toward Simplifying Application Development, in a Dozen Lessons."
21. Shibata, "How to Build a Platform Team Now!"
22. Shibata, "How to Build a Platform Team Now!"
23. Beer, *Brain of the Firm*, 238.
24. Shibata, "How to Build a Platform Team Now!"
25. Hall, "ITSM, DevOps, and Why Three-Tier Support Should Be Replaced with Swarming."
26. Forsgren et al., *Accelerate*, 68.

Chapter 6

1. Forsgren et al., *Accelerate*, 63.
2. Forsgren et al., *Accelerate*, 66.
3. Bernstein and Turban, "The Impact of the 'Open' Workspace on Human Collaboration."
4. Evans, *Domain-Driven Design*.
5. Fowler, "Bliki: BoundedContext."

6. Tune and Millett, *Designing Autonomous Teams and Services*, 38.
7. Nygard, "The Perils of Semantic Coupling."
8. Helfand, *Dynamic Reteaming*, 203.
9. Hering, *DevOps for the Modern Enterprise*, 45.
10. Phillips, "Testing Observability."

Chapter 7

1. Bernstein et al., "How Intermittent Breaks in Interaction Improve Collective Intelligence," 8734–8739.
2. Rother, *Toyota Kata*, 236.
3. Kim and Pierce, "Convergent Versus Divergent Thinking," 245–250.
4. Urquhart, "Communications and Conway's Law."
5. Betz, *Managing Digital*, 253.
6. Burgess, *Thinking in Promises*, 105.
7. Reinertsen, *The Principles of Product Development Flow*, 233.
8. Malan, "Conway's Law."
9. Kelly, "Return to Conway's Law."
10. Helfand, *Dynamic Reteaming*, 121; Wiley, as quoted in Helfand, *Dynamic Reteaming*, 121.
11. Helfand, *Dynamic Reteaming*, 13.
12. Reinertsen, *The Principles of Product Development Flow*, 254.

Chapter 8

1. Forsgren et al., *Accelerate*, 63.
2. Ingles, "Convergence to Kubernetes."
3. Ingles, "Convergence to Kubernetes,"
4. Sussna, *Designing Delivery*, 61.
5. Kotter, "Accelerate!"
6. Drucker, *The Daily Drucker*, 291.
7. Stanford, *Guide to Organisation Design*, 17.
8. Narayan, *Agile IT Organization Design*, 65.
9. Kim et al., *The DevOps Handbook*, 11.
10. Sussna, *Designing Delivery*, 58.
11. Narayan, *Agile IT Organization Design*, 31.

Conclusion

1. Conway, "How do Committees Invent?" 31.
2. Manns and Rising, *Fearless Change*.

INDEX

ACKNOWLEDGMENTS

Writing a book is a collaborative task involving many people without whom the finished book wouldn't be impossible. We'd like to thank our peer reviewers for taking the time to give detailed feedback on the book: Charles T. Betz, Jeremy Brown, Joanne Molesky, Nick Tune, and Ruth Malan. We also want to thank the authors and originators of our case studies and industry examples: Albert Bertilsson, Anders Ivarsson, Andy Humphrey, Andy Rubio, Damien Daly, Dave Hotchkiss, Dave Whyte, Eric Minick, Fernando Cornago, Gustaf Nilsson Kotte, Henrik Kniberg, Ian Watson, Markus Rautert, Michael Lambert, Michael Maibaum, Miguel Antunes, Paul Ingles, Pulak Agrawal, Robin Weston, Stephanie Sheehan, and Wolfgang John.

We'd like to thank everyone who contributed to the original DevOps Topologies patterns, especially James Betteley, Jamie Buchanan, John Clapham, Kevin Hinde, and Matt Franz. A special thanks goes to John Cutler for a passionate outsider's view of the Team Topologies approach, and to Gareth Rushgrove for helping to expand the audience for the original DevOps Topologies patterns. We also want to thank our colleague Jovile Bartkeviciute at Conflux for her tireless research.

The team at IT Revolution Press has been amazing, especially Anna Noak, Lean Brown, and the other editors and designers—we've really valued their advice, support, and infectious enthusiasm. We're grateful to Gene Kim for inviting us to speak at DevOps Enterprise Summit in London in 2017, which helped us to realize the value of the emerging Team Topologies ideas.

Finally, we'd like to thank the people whose ideas, talks, and writing inspired us to become interested in the fascinating relationship between teams and software in the first place, and helped to make this book a reality: Allan Kelly, Andy Longshaw, Charles T. Betz, Donella Meadows, James Lewis, Gene Kim, Mel Conway, Mirco Hering, Rachel Laycock, Ruth Malan, and Randy Shoup.

ABOUT THE AUTHORS

Matthew Skelton has been building, deploying, and operating commercial software systems since 1998, and has worked for organizations including London Stock Exchange, GlaxoSmithKline, FT.com, LexisNexis, and the UK government. Head of Consulting at Conflux (confluxdigital.net), Matthew is the co-author of the books *Continuous Delivery with Windows and .NET* (2016) and *Team Guide to Software Operability* (2016). Matthew holds a BSc in computer science and cybernetics from the University of Reading, an MSc in neuroscience from the University of Oxford, and an MA in music from the Open University; he is a chartered engineer (CEng) in the UK. In his free time, Matthew plays the trumpet, sings in choirs, writes music, and enjoys trail running.

Manuel Pais is an independent DevOps and Continuous Delivery Consultant focused on team design, practices, and flow. He helps organizations define and adopt DevOps and Continuous Delivery (both from technical and human perspectives) via strategic assessments, practical workshops, and coaching. Manuel is the co-author of *Team Guide to Software Releasability* (2018).

Matthew and **Manuel** have worked together on organization design for modern software systems with many clients around the world. Their training sessions on organization design for modern software systems have helped numerous organizations to rethink their approach to team intercommunication and software architecture, improving flow and the effectiveness of software delivery.